Quick Clicks

REFERENCE GUIDE

MICROSOFT®

EXCEL® 2007

CAREERTRACK.

CAROL HERBERT

QuickClicks Excel 2007 Reference Guide

1st Edition

Litho U.S.A.

Distributed in the U.S. and Canada

For orders or more information, please contact our customer service department at
1-800-556-3009

ISBN: 978-1-935041-50-4

Item # 32013

Trademarks

Disclaimer

The *QuickClicks Reference Guide* series is dedicated to all of CareerTrack's devoted customers. Our customers' commitment to continuing education and professional development inspired the creation of the award-winning *Unlocking the Secrets* CD-ROM series and the *QuickClicks Reference Guide* series. Thank you for your continued support!

Contents

Introduction vi
    Find Your Way Around viii

Get to Know

1   Customize Your Excel Environment 2
2   Adjust Row Height and Column Width 4
3   Hide and Unhide Columns and Rows 8
4   Freeze and Unfreeze Columns and Rows 10
5   Choose a File Format when Saving a Workbook 12

Format

6   Merge and Unmerge Cells 14
7   Create Your Own Cell Style or Format 16
8   Copy Styles to Other Workbooks 18
9   Convert Text to Numbers 20
10   Apply Simple Formatting to Numbers, Dates, and Times 24
11   Apply Advanced Formatting to Numbers, Dates, and Times 26

Calculate

12   Name a Cell For Use in Formulas and Functions 30
13   Insert Subtotals 32
14   Insert a Basic Formula 36
15   Copy a Formula to Multiple Cells 40
16   Calculate the Difference Between Two Times 42
17   Count the Number of Work Days Between Two Dates 46
18   Insert a Basic Function 48
19   Use Conditional Functions 52
20   Troubleshoot Formula and Function Errors 56
21   Find Formulas, Functions, and Cells Connected to a Cell 58
22   Calculate Percentages in a PivotTable 60
23   Create a PivotTable Calculated Field 64
24   Create a PivotTable Calculated Item 66

Analyze

25   Use Data Filters 70
26   Highlight Cells Based on Specific Criteria 72
27   Use Graphics to Compare Cell Values 76
28   Create a PivotTable 80
29   Delete a PivotTable 84
30   Change How Data is Displayed in a PivotTable 86
31   Group Data within a PivotTable 86
32   Find a Value From Another Table 94

Automate

33 Find the Tab that Allows Access to Macros and VBA 98

34 Record a Macro 100

35 Bookmark Cells and Groups of Cells for Easy Reference 104

Illustrate

36 Insert a Chart 106

37 Determine if Your Data Shows a Relevant Trend 110

38 Create a Chart From Your PivotTable 114

39 Insert a SmartArt Graphic 118

40 Configure a SmartArt Graphic 120

41 Select and Apply a Themes to Your Document 122

42 Make Your Own Theme. 126

43 Add Information to the Tops or Bottoms of Printed Pages. 128

44 Page Setup. 130

45 Choose Which Part of Your Worksheet to Print 134

46 Print Multiple Worksheets 138

47 Print to a Specific Number of Pages 140

Collaborate

48 Link Worksheets Together 144

49 Prepare Your Spreadsheet Data for Use in Access 148

50 Pull Data from a Website or Network Location 152

51 Personalize and Customize Documents 156

Accelerate

52 Customize the Quick Access Toolbar 160

53 Choose What is Transferred When You Cut/Copy and Paste. 164

54 Save a Workbook as a Template 166

55 Create Your Own Fillable List of Items 168

56 Use Autofill to Quickly Fill Cells from a List 170

Appendices

A Excel or Access: Which Do I Need?. 172

B Chart Terminology 178

C Formulas and Functions 182

D Keyboard Shortcuts 186

Index 192

Introduction

Congratulations on your purchase of *QuickClicks: Microsoft Excel 2007*. You have invested wisely in yourself and taken a step forward with regard to your personal and professional development.

This reference guide is an important tool in your productivity toolbox and will help you work more efficiently and effectively when using Microsoft Excel. Each tip was carefully selected based on how often the feature results in additional assistance and how much time and effort it saves you.

Anatomy of a Tip

Each page displays the tip's title so you always know where you are and what you are learning about.

Each tip has been assigned a difficulty value of between one and four, with one circle representing the easiest tips and four circles representing the hardest.

Difficulty:

All tips begin with an explanation, which includes a description of the feature and how the feature might be used in a business setting. A set of easy-to-follow numbered Step-by-Step instructions follow with lettered callouts that point to important parts of the instructions on illustrations. The displayed names of all selections and buttons are bolded, which makes them easy for you to find.

Many tips include bonus information and suggestions. In some cases, a miniature version of the icon appears at the end of a sentence or step, which indicates that a shaded box (with a matching icon) appears at the end of the tip. If there are multiple bonus features, they are in the order in which they appeared in the text.

The titles and tips are written in plain English, which makes it easy for you to find what you want to do. Where appropriate, the tips include "What Microsoft Calls It" references, so you can learn the lingo and perform more effective searches for additional feature capabilities in Microsoft's help system.

 What Microsoft Calls It:

Extras include the following:

Icon	Name	What it Means
	Bright Idea	Bright Ideas provide additional information that you might not know about Excel or about the feature in question.
	Hot Tip	Hot Tips are functions or features related to the one being taught or include additional uses for the features and functions.
	Caution	Cautions indicate those situations where you might find yourself tripped up by a particularly complicated operation, instances when making an incorrect choice will cause you more work to correct, or times when very similar options might be confusing.

There are two other tips that do not have miniature icons in-line followed by full explanations at the end. These are special features.

Icon	Name	What it Means
	Options	Options represent places where there are two or more ways to accomplish a task, or where two or more results might be obtainable, depending on the choices you make. Option icons appear within the text and all relevant choices are next to the icon.
	Quickest Click	Quickest Clicks indicate there is a quicker way to accomplish the same task taught in the tip. Shortcuts like this, though, often leave out important steps that help you understand what you are doing. Because of this, each tip teaches the most complete method for accomplishing a task, and a Quickest Click appears if there is a quicker option.

At the bottom of each page, you will see either a Continue or a Stop icon. These icons indicate if the tip continues on the next page or if it is complete.

Find Your Way Around

Items You'll See in the Excel Window

The tips are written in plain English, but it is hard to get completely away from using some technical terms. What follows are three maps that show you what this book calls various features in Microsoft Excel.

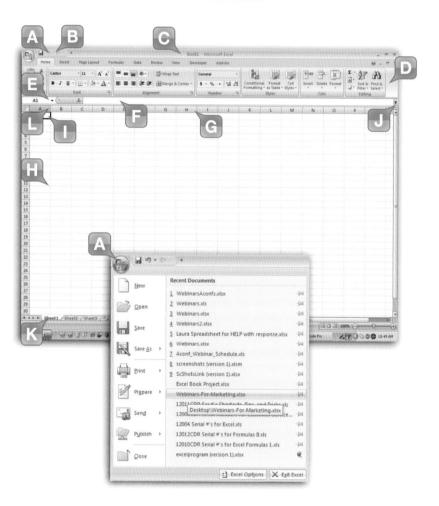

The Excel Window

A Office Button and Menu	Click this button to access the Windows Menu. Find open, save, and print options, pinned documents, and the Excel Options button.
B Quick Launch Bar	Place items here for quick and easy access.
C Title Bar	View the title and file type of the active document.
D Ribbon	Locate Excel menu items and controls.
E Name Box	Give a cell a name.
F Formula Bar	Enter data or type a formula or function.
G Column Headers	Click to select an entire column or use the letter in formulas and functions.
H Row Headers	Click to select an entire row or use the number in formulas and functions.
I Active Cell	The black border indicates the currently active cell or range.
J Formula Bar Expander	Expand the formula bar to view long formulas and functions.
K Sheet Tabs and Navigation Controls	These allow you to select sheets, move between sheets, and add/delete sheets.
L Select Sheet Button	Click to select the entire active sheet.

Items You'll See on the Ribbon

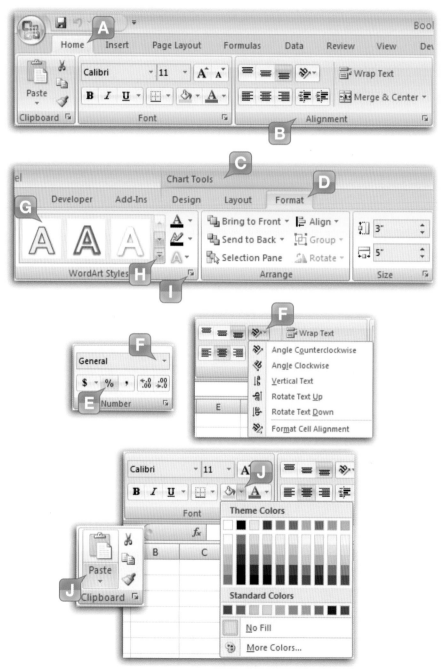

Items You'll See on the Ribbon

A Tab	Collections of related features and functions.
B Group	Collections of related controls.
C Highlighted Ribbon Section	Contextual ribbon sections appear when some items are selected or used.
D Contextual Tabs	Some specialized tabs only appear when a particular feature is active. These special tabs usually appear in conjunction with a highlighted ribbon section.
E Buttons	Buttons are single-click controls that perform one function.
F Dropdown Menus and Dropdown Buttons	Some buttons have a graphic and a down-pointing arrow, while others have a default selection visible, followed by a down arrow. Clicking the arrow reveals additional choices.
G Selection Box	A panel containing a list of selectable items.
H Panel Launcher	A scroll control that can be clicked to launch a selection panel.
I Dialog Box Launcher	A special group control that launches a related dialog box.
J Combo Button	These controls are split into two parts to function as both a button and a dropdown. They may be split horizontally or vertically.

Items You'll See in Menus and Dialog Boxes

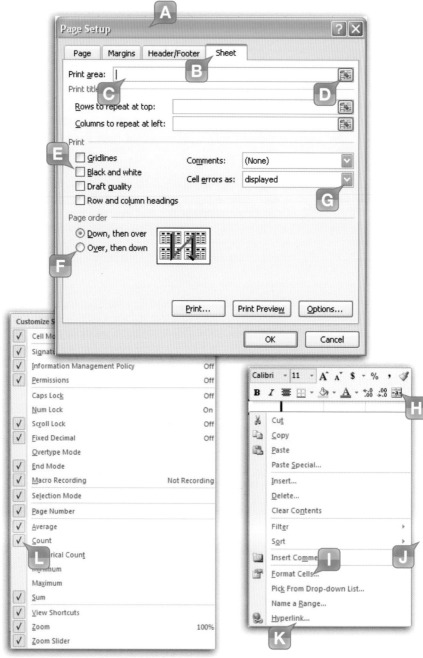

Items You'll See in Menus and Dialog Boxes

A Dialog Box	A feature-specific box that you can launch to control various functions in Excel.
B Tabs	Some dialog boxes have tabs similar to the ones on the ribbon. Each tab is focused on a particular subset of features.
C Textbox	A box where text can be typed.
D Selection Tool	A button that, when pressed, minimizes the dialog box that houses it and allows direct selection of cells.
E Checkbox	A box that activates the related selection when checked and deactivates it when unchecked. More than one checkbox may be checked in a series.
F Radio Button	A circle that activates the related selection when selected and deactivates it when deselected. Only one radio button may be selected in a series.
G Dropdown Menu	A simple down-pointing arrow button that reveals a set of selectable choices.
H Right-Click Menu	This two-part menu appears when you right-click anywhere on the sheet.
I Dialog Box Launcher	In menus, selections that launch dialog boxes are followed by ellipses (…).
J Menu Launcher	Menu selections that open additional menus are followed by right-pointing arrows.
K Shortcut Keys	Menu selections that can be launched by a keystroke on your keyboard can be identified by the underlined letters in them. Click any underlined letter in a menu to launch that selection's function.
L Toggle Checkmarks	Some menus have checkmarks. Clicking an unchecked item in those lists checks it and activates the selected option. Clicking a checked item unchecks it and deactivates the selected option.

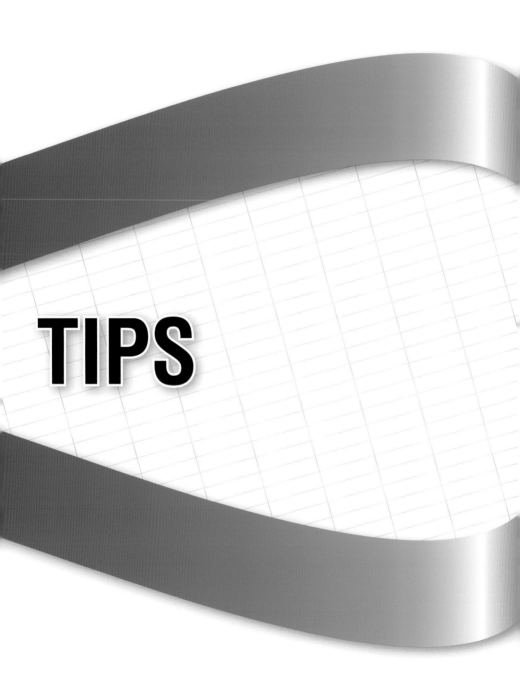

TIPS

1 Customize Your Excel Environment

Difficulty:

There will be times when the way Excel is set up by default does not match your personal work style or the needs of your company or industry. Because Excel is designed to enhance productivity, Microsoft has provided ways for organizations and users to customize their workspaces and experience.

Some customization is achieved by adding options to the **Quick Access Toolbar** or the **Action Bar**, but the most robust changes are accessible from the **Excel Options** screens.

> **What Microsoft Calls It:** Customize User Preferences

SEE ALSO: CUSTOMIZE THE QUICK ACCESS TOOLBAR

 Step-by-Step

Set User Preferences in Excel

1. Click the **Office** button **A**.

2. Click the **Excel Options** button **B**.

3. Make adjustments to the various sections **C**.

   - **Popular**: Change the most-often modified settings within Excel, including Custom Lists, default workbook settings and personalizing your copy of Excel.

- **Formulas**: Adjust options related to formula calculation, performance and error handling.

- **Proofing**: Modify how Excel corrects and formats text.

- **Save**: Decide how and how often workbooks are saved.

- **Advanced**: Modify additional Excel settings. Note that many of the settings adjusted here have ramifications that should be carefully considered before changes are made.

- **Customize**: Add/remove items to/from the **Quick Access Toolbar**.

- **Add-Ins**: Manage your Excel **Add-Ins**. Note that most installed **Add-Ins** will not appear on the **Add-Ins** tab unless they are active.

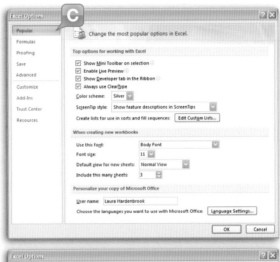

- **Trust Center**: Manage workbook security settings.

- **Resources**: Access a variety of resources and links to use Excel to its fullest potential.

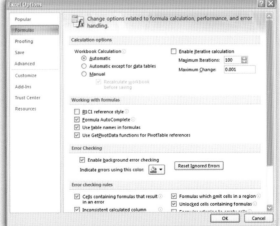

4. Click the **Save** button.

2 | Adjust Row Height and Column Width

Difficulty: ●○○○

Cells can hold a lot of information and sometimes you need to see all of that information at a glance.

In columns, long strings or passages of text are often truncated **A** or appear to have spilled into the next cell **B**. Numbers appear as "#" signs **C** if there is not enough room to display them in full.

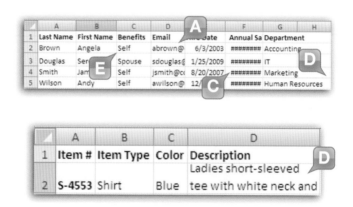

In rows, sometimes you can tell there needs to be more space **D**, but sometimes you can't tell. In the Benefits column **E** of the illustration there are multiple rows of text hidden by the inadequate row height.

By adjusting the widths of the columns and the heights of the rows, improve the appearance *and* usability of your spreadsheet.

There are two methods that can be used to adjust row height and column width:

- **Use the Mouse:** Click and drag to make adjustments using your eyes as a guide for the appropriate size.

- **Use the Format Menu:** Adjust the width in a dialog box.

Step-by-Step

Use the Mouse. Use this option when you need to change a few rows or columns to accommodate longer cell data.

1. Click a numbered row header 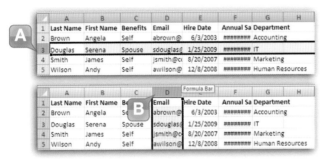 or lettered column header **B** to select that row/column for adjustment.

2. Move the pointer to the right border of a selected column's header (or the bottom border of a selected row's header) until the pointer changes into a plus sign with up and down or right and left arrowheads (↕ ↔) **C**.

3. Click and drag the border right or left (or up or down) to the width (or height) you desire. As you drag, the new border is identified by a dotted line **D** and the current measurement displays in a message box **E**.

4. Release the mouse when you are at the desired width.

CONTINUE

2 Adjust Row Height and Column Width (continued)

Step-by-Step

Use the Format Menu. Use this option when you need to adjust row height (or column width) for many rows or an entire sheet.

1. Select the rows you want to adjust. 💧

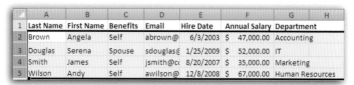

2. On the **Home** tab, click the **Format** button **A** in the **Cells** group.

3. Select **Row Height** **B**. The **Row Height** dialog appears. (This dialog can also be accessed by right-clicking on a cell.)

4. Enter in a new height value in points (there are 72 points to an inch) in the **Row height** textbox **C**.

5. Click the **OK** button **D**.

6. This adjusts all rows to the same height, regardless of the amount of information in each cell.

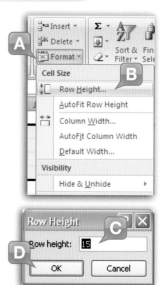

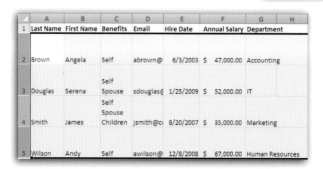

Bright Idea: To select more than one adjacent row or column, click and drag to make your selections. To select more than one non-adjacent row or column, hold the **CTRL** key while you click row headers to select your rows.

Hot Tip: Select an entire sheet by clicking the **Sheet Selection button** ( ) 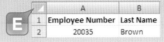 or by pressing **CTRL+A** on your keyboard.

	A	B
1	Employee Number	Last Name
2	20035	Brown

Quickest Click: Fit row height or column width to match the contents of the cells in an entire selection at once. To do so, first select the cells to adjust. Next, move the pointer to the space between any two row or column headers until you see it change to a plus sign with arrows ( ), then double-click. The rows/columns automatically adjust to fit the content.

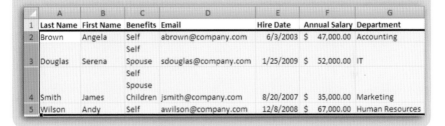

	A	B	C	D	E	F	G
1	Last Name	First Name	Benefits	Email	Hire Date	Annual Salary	Department
2	Brown	Angela	Self	abrown@company.com	6/3/2003	$ 47,000.00	Accounting
3	Douglas	Serena	Self Spouse	sdouglas@company.com	1/25/2009	$ 52,000.00	IT
4	Smith	James	Self Spouse Children	jsmith@company.com	8/20/2007	$ 35,000.00	Marketing
5	Wilson	Andy	Self	awilson@company.com	12/8/2008	$ 67,000.00	Human Resources

3 Hide and Unhide Columns and Rows

Difficulty:

There are times when you may want to hide columns or rows in your worksheet. Information may be confidential or irrelevant to those who use the sheet. You don't want to lose the data, you want to make it invisible. The **Hide/Unhide** feature accomplishes this goal.

In the example below, the Annual Salary column has been hidden from view. 🔥

	A	B	C	D	E	F
1	Last Name	First Name	Benefits	Hire Date	Annual Salary	Department
2	Brown	Angela	Self	6/3/2003	$ 47,000.00	Accounting
3	Douglas	Serena	Self Spouse	1/25/2009	$ 52,000.00	IT
4	Smith	James	Self Spouse Children	8/20/2007	$ 35,000.00	Marketing
5	Wilson	Andy	Self	12/8/2008	$ 67,000.00	Human Resources

	A	B	C	D	F
1	Last Name	First Name	Benefits	Hire Date	Department
2	Brown	Angela	Self	6/3/2003	Accounting
3	Douglas	Serena	Self Spouse	1/25/2009	IT
4	Smith	James	Self Spouse Children	8/20/2007	Marketing
5	Wilson	Andy	Self	12/8/2008	Human Resources

 **Step-by-Step**

Hide/Unhide Columns or Rows

1. Click the lettered column header or numbered row header of the columns or rows to be hidden **A**. *Note: When Unhiding, you need to select the columns/rows adjacent to the hidden one.* 💡

2. Click on the **Home** tab.

3. In the **Cells** panel, click the **Format** button and then select **Hide & Unhide** and your selection .

- **Hide Rows**: Hides the selected row(s).

- **Hide Columns**: Hides the selected column(s).

- **Hide Sheet**: Hides the whole active worksheet.

- **Unhide Rows**: Unhides any hidden rows within the selected area.

- **Unhide Columns**: Unhides any hidden columns within the selected area.

Hot Tip: Hide an entire worksheet by right-clicking its tab and selecting **Hide** from the fly-out menu that appears.

To select more than one adjacent row or column, click and drag to make your selections. To select more than one non-adjacent row or column, hold the key while you click row headers to select your rows.

Quickest Click: Select the columns or rows you want to hide. Right-click your selection and choose **Hide** or **Unhide** from the right-click menu .

4 Freeze and Unfreeze Columns and Rows

Difficulty: ●○○○

When you are working with an extremely large worksheet, you may find that when you have scrolled down or right to the data you want to review, you can't recall which column or row contains the data you need. The answer is to freeze columns and rows so they are always visible, even when you scroll.

Freezing columns keeps them visible while you scroll to the right. Freezing rows keeps them visible while you scroll down. By freezing the first column **A**, you can keep headers, like employee numbers, in place as you look for data in some of the far right columns of the spreadsheet.

Likewise, by freezing the first row **B**, you can keep row headers, like employee data categories, in place as you scroll down in your spreadsheet. **⚠**

	A	B	C	D
1	Employee Number	Last Name	First Name	Benefits
2	20035	Brown	Angela	Self
3	26829	Douglas	Serena	Self Spouse
4	22563	Franklin	Edna	Self

A

	A	E	F	G	H
1	Employee Number	Hire Date	Annual Salary	Dept.	Street Addres
2	20035	6/3/2003	$ 47,000.00	Acctg.	7750 Elm C
3	26829	1/25/2009	$ 52,000.00	IT	22398 Bria
4	22563	8/7/2004	$ 33,000.00	Sales	4332 W. El

	A	B	C	D
1	Employee Number	Last Name	First Name	Benefits
5	24389	Hawkins	Rory	-
6	24556	Johnson	Kim	Self
7	10123	Smith	James	Self Spouse Children
8	10086	Wilson	Andy	Self

B

Step-by-Step

Freeze a Column or a Row

1. Place your cursor in the cell to the right and/or below where you want the freezing lines to be drawn.

    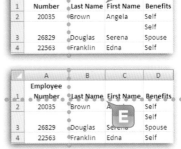

    - Click cell A2 **C** to freeze the top row.

    - Click cell B1 **D** to freeze the first column.

    - Click cell B2 **E** to freeze the the top row and the left column.

    - Click cell A1 to freeze your sheet along vertical and horizontal midpoints.

    - Click in any other cell to freeze all rows above and columns to the left of the selection.

2. On the **View** tab in the **Window** group, click the **Freeze Panes** dropdown and select **Freeze Panes**.

Unfreezing Columns and Rows

On the **View** tab in the **Window** group, click the **Freeze Panes** dropdown and select **Unfreeze Panes**.

 Caution: At first it can be tricky to figure out which cell to click to freeze the right rows and columns. Try it a few times, freezing and unfreezing, until you get the hang of it.

 Quickest Click: Freeze the Top Row or First Column
You can quickly freeze the top row or left column by selecting the **Freeze Top Row** or **Freeze First Column** options from the **Freeze Panes** dropdown in the **Window** group of the **View** tab.

5 Choose a File Format When Saving a Workbook

Difficulty: ●○○○

When you are saving a document (or a copy of a document) for others to use or to meet specific requirements, use the **Save As** command rather than simply hitting the **Save** button on the **Quick Access** toolbar (or in the **Windows** menu).

Collaborating with people who have different versions of Excel, security concerns, tracking changes, preparing data for export, or readying your worksheet for inclusion on a web page are all reasons you might need to save your file as something other than a standard 2007 .XLSX file.

Microsoft offers you many options when it comes to file types and formats, each with its own purposes.

Step-by-Step

Choose a File Format When Saving a Workbook

1. Click on the **Office Button** **A**.

2. Click **Save As** **B**.

3. Select one of the available options, or choose **Other Formats** **C**. Any of these choices causes the **Save As** dialog box **D** to appear.

4. Type in a file name for your workbook in the **File name** text box E.

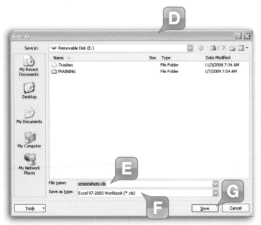

5. Select a file type from the **Save as Type** dropdown menu F (if you selected an option rather than **Other Formats**, the dropdown is populated with your selection).

- **Excel Workbook**: .XLSX This is the default 2007 file format.

- **Excel Macro-Enabled Workbook**: .XLSM This format is essentially the same as the default format, except that it can store VBA code. If you include VBA code you will be prompted to save in this format. .XLTM is the template version of this format.

- **Excel Binary Workbook**: .XLSB This is the fastest-loading file format and accommodates VBA. It is not, however, an XML format and is not ideal for data management without Excel 2007. There are also security concerns associated with this format.

- **Excel 97-2003 Workbook**: .XLS This is a format fully accessible by previous versions of Excel back to 97. The .XLT format, 97-2003 template, is also available.

- **Other Formats**: Other formats are available, such as .HTML (for the web), .TXT (text only), and .CSV (Comma Separated Value).

6. Click the **Save** button G.

Choose a File Format When Saving a Workbook   **13**

6 | Merge and Unmerge Cells

Difficulty:

There may be times when you want to merge cells across rows and columns.

For example, when working with sheets that contain several different types of information and/or the sheets are used by multiple people or groups, it is helpful to label various areas of the sheet or collections of data.

There are several options for merging, all found in the **Merge and Split** menu **A** accessed from the **Merge & Center** dropdown button in the **Alignment** group of the **Home** tab.

- **Merge & Center**: Merges selected cells and centers cell contents in the resulting cell.

- **Merge Across**: Merges selected cells into rows along existing row dividers and left-justifies cell contents in the resulting cell(s).

- **Merge Cells**: Merges cells across column and row dividers and left-justifies cell contents in the resulting cell.

- **Unmerge Cells**: Unmerges all merged cells in the selected areas.

Merging and splitting cells works differently in Excel than it does in other Microsoft Office programs. While helpful, the operations have more rules and consequences and therefore require a bit more planning. ⚠

Step-by-Step

Merge Cells

1. Select the cells you want to merge .

2. On the **Home** tab, click the **Merge & Center** button 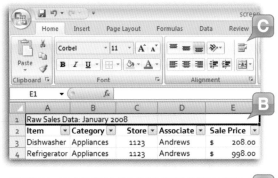 in the **Alignment** group.

3. Review your merged data 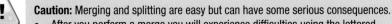.

Split a Merged Cell

1. Select the merged cell you want to split.

2. On the **Home** tab, click the **Merge & Center** button in the **Alignment** group.

3. Click **Unmerge**.

> **Caution:** Merging and splitting are easy but can have some serious consequences.
> - After you perform a merge you will experience difficulties using the lettered headers to select an entire column, or the numbered headers to select an entire row. You can still use the **CTRL** and **SHIFT** keys to select several cells, but you will no longer be able to select large regions around the merge with a single click.
> - If you attempt to merge cells that contain data, you may receive an error warning you that some of the cell contents will be lost.
> - When unmerging merged cells, you need to perform one split at a time to avoid data loss.

7 | Create Your Own Style or Format

Difficulty:

Excel includes many options to control the appearance of numbers, text, and cells. **Styles**, pre-set formats, streamline the formatting process to quickly apply a consistent look across all of your workbooks. Forcing data into a single format— such as formatting all of your dates to read "11/24/74" rather than "November 24, 1974" or "1974/11/24"—means that no matter how people enter the information, it will be reformatted for clarity. Consistency means fewer errors, a unified and professional look and at-a-glance answers.

	A	B	C	D
1	Last Name	First Name	Hire Date	Annual Salary
2	Brown	Angela	6/3/2003	$ 47,000.00
3	Douglas	Serena	1/25/2009	$ 52,000.00
4	Franklin	Edna	8/7/2004	$ 33,000.00
5	Hawkins	Rory	9/16/2004	$ 22,000.00

	A	B	C
1	Store Number	Transaction Date	Amount
2	1123	Sunday, February 01, 2009	$ 15.00
3	1123	Wednesday, January 03, 2007	$ 3.00
4	1123	Wednesday, January 03, 2007	$ 2.75
5	1123	Wednesday, January 03, 2007	$ 22.00

View and use a wide range of pre-set styles available in Excel with the **Style Gallery**, accessed via the **Cell Styles** button in the **Styles** group of the **Home** tab. Even with the wide variety of provided styles, there are times when you want to create your own. 💡

SEE ALSO: COPY STYLES TO OTHER WORKBOOKS

> 💬 **What Microsoft Calls it:** Custom Styles

🪜 Step-by-Step

Create a Custom Style

1. Format a cell and its contents the way you would like to save as a **Custom Style**. Settings include: Number, Alignment, Font, Border, Fill, and Protection.

	A	B	C	D	E	F
1	Employee Number	Last Name	First Name	Benefits	Hire D	Annual Salary
2	20035	Brown	Angela	Self	6/3/2003	$ 47,000.00
3	26829	Douglas	Serena	Self Spouse	1/25/2009	$ 52,000.00
4	22563	Franklin	Edna	Self	8/7/2004	$ 33,000.00

2. Select your formatted cell .

3. Click the **Cell Styles** button in the **Styles** group of the **Home** tab to open the **Style Gallery**.

4. Click on **New Cell Style** at the bottom of the **Style Gallery**.

5. Type in a name for your **Custom Style** in the **Style name** textbox of the **Style** dialog box.

6. Click the **OK** button.

Bright Idea: Use the **Format Painter**, accessed via the **Format Painter** button in the **Clipboard** group of the **Home** tab, to apply styles.

8 | Copy Styles to Other Workbooks

Difficulty:

Once you have established styles for your workbook—whether they are standard Microsoft styles or custom styles you have developed yourself—you can copy them from one workbook to any other workbook. This saves you time since you don't need to spend hours re-creating the look and feel with which you and other users are familiar. 🔥

SEE ALSO: CREATE YOUR OWN STYLE OR FORMAT

Step-by-Step

Copy a Style to Another Workbook

1. Open the file containing the **Custom Style** to copy to another workbook.

2. Open the workbook to which you wish to copy the selected **Custom Style**.

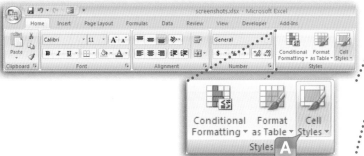

3. Click the **Cell Styles** button **A** in the **Styles** group of the **Home** tab to open the **Style Gallery** **B**. Select **Merge Styles** **C** at the bottom of the **Style Gallery** to open the **Merge Styles** dialog box **D**.

4. Select the workbook that contains the styles you want to copy .

5. Click the **OK** button.

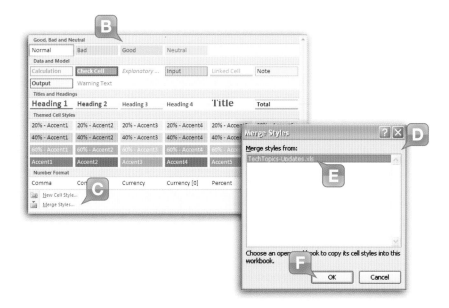

  Hot Tip: You don't have to copy each style individually. When you copy styles from one workbook to another, Excel pulls all saved styles at once.

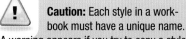 **Caution:** Each style in a work-book must have a unique name. A warning appears if you try to copy a style into a workbook that already contains a style with the same name. If you want to replace the existing style with the new one of the same name, click **Yes**. If not, click **No** and rename the styles before attempting the merge again.

9 Convert Text to Numbers

Difficulty:

When data is transferred from external sources into Excel, numbers can be mistaken for text. While this might not be a problem most of the time, you will find that it can cause some notation **A** and formula **B** errors. To avoid or correct this problem, convert the text to numbers.

Excel provides two options to accomplish the conversion: Reformat the cells as numbers, or multiply each cell by one using the **Paste Special** function. The first option is fastest, but occasionally creates irregularities (often as a result of how the data was entered originally). The second option takes longer but produces more consistent results.

SEE ALSO: APPLY SIMPLE FORMATTING TO NUMBERS, DATES, AND TIMES; APPLY ADVANCED FORMATTING TO NUMBERS, DATES, AND TIMES

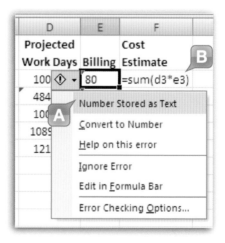

Step-by-Step

Convert Data with the Paste Special Function

Use this method to ensure the data is correctly converted for use in formulas and equations.

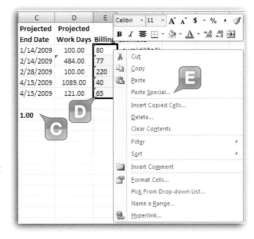

1. Enter "1" into any nearby empty cell **C**. Format that cell as a number.

2. Right-click the cell containing the "1" and select **Copy**, or press **CTRL+C** on your keyboard.

3. Select the cells you want to convert **D**.

4. Right-click the selection and choose **Paste Special E** to launch the **Paste Special** dialog box **F**.

5. Click on the **Multiply** radio button **G**.

6. Click the **OK** button. 🔥

CONTINUE

Convert Text to Numbers   21

9 Convert Text to Numbers (continued)

Hot Tip: You may need to re-enter any formulas that were broken because of the columns that were formatted as text. Once you have re-entered them they should work **H**.

C	D	E	F
Projected End Date	Projected Work Days	Billing	Cost Estimate
1/14/2009	10.00	80	$ 800.00
2/14/2009	22.00	77	$ 1,694.00
2/28/2009	10.00	220	$ 2,200.00
4/15/2009	33.00	40	$ 1,320.00
4/15/2009	11.00	65	$ 715.00
1.00			

Quickest Click: Reformat Using the Numbers Group or the Format Cells Dialog Box

Select the cells you want to convert, then click the number format dropdown  in the **Numbers** group of the **Home** tab and select **Number** . You may also choose to right-click the selection and select **Format Cells** or press **CTRL+1** on the keyboard to open the **Format Cells** dialog box. Once you have the dialog box open, use the options on the **Number** tab to make your adjustments.

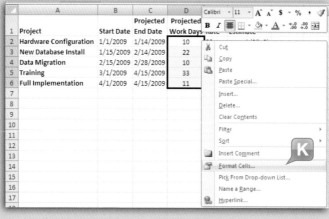

10 | Apply Simple Formatting to Numbers, Dates, and Times

Difficulty:  ⬤◯◯◯

Excel provides a multitude of formatting options for customizing numbers, dates and times. These options allow you to present data in the way that best expresses your needs and to conform with any government, industry or company standards and styles that might apply to your data.

SEE ALSO: CONVERT TEXT TO NUMBERS; APPLY ADVANCED FORMATTING TO NUMBERS, DATES, AND TIMES

⌐ Step-by-Step

Apply a Simple Number Format via the Numbers Group Controls

1. Select your cells to be formatted.

2. On the **Home** tab, select a format button from the **Numbers** panel  or click the numbers format dropdown **B** to choose from additional options.

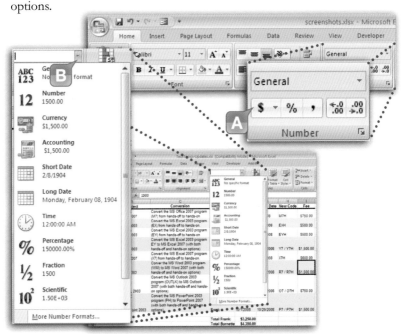

- **Currency Combo Button**: Click the left half of the button—the half with the symbol—to format the selected cells as currency (100 becomes $100.00). Click the right half of the button—the one with the down arrow—to see more currency and accounting formatting options.

- **Percentage Button**: Click this button to append each number in the selected cells with a % sign.

- **Comma Button**: Click this button to add comma separators to each number in the selected cells and append each number with a decimal point followed by two decimal places (1000 becomes 1,000.00).

- **Decimal Adjuster Buttons**: Click these buttons to add or remove decimal places, one at a time, from numbers (3.14 becomes 3.1 or 3.140).

Bright Idea: You can apply formatting to cells before they contain any data. By setting up your formatting before you—or anyone else—enters data into the sheet, you guarantee that formatting will be consistent and make entering the data faster and easier.

11

Apply Advanced Formatting to Numbers, Dates, and Times

Difficulty: ●○○○

When the pre-set number formatting options available in the **Number** group or the **Number** dropdown do not meet your needs, use the options in the **Format Cells** dialog box to create the formatting you desire.

See Also: Convert Text to Numbers; Apply Simple Formatting to Numbers, Dates, and Times

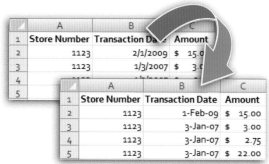

Step-by-Step

Apply a Date Format via the Format Cells Dialog

1. Select the cells to which you want to apply the custom format.

2. On the **Home** tab in the **Number** group, click the **Format Cell**s dialog box launcher **A** to open the **Format Cells** dialog box.

3. Click on the **Number** tab **B**.

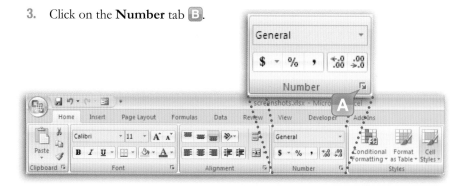

4. Click on **Date** C in the **Category** pane.

5. Select the specific format you want from the **Type** combo box D.

6. Click the **OK** button E.

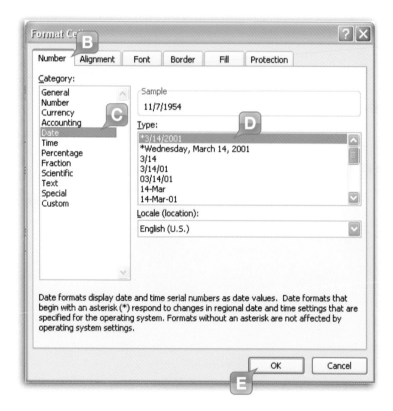

Step-by-Step

Apply a Time Format via the Format Cells Dialog

Use this method to apply custom date or time formatting to your data.

1. Select the cells to which you want to apply the custom format.

2. Open the **Format Cells** dialog box.

3. Click on the **Number** tab.

4. Click on **Time** in the **Category** pane.

5. Select the specific format you want from the **Type** combo box.

6. Select your location in the **Local (location)** dropdown. This selection determines how the time is displayed (such as whether midnight is 12:00:00 AM or 00:00:00 AM).

7. Click the **OK** button.

Hot Tip: If you are not in the U.S., or are preparing your sheet for international use, select your location in the **Local (location)** dropdown. This changes the formats available in the **Type** combo box to match those appropriate to your region.

Bright Idea: Use the **Text** category to convert numbers to text. This selection allows you to begin numbers with zeroes (00934), which number formats will not permit. Once converted, the text numbers should not be used in calculations.

12 | Name a Value for Use in Formulas and Functions

Difficulty: ●●○○

You can save time and effort and reduce errors by applying a named value to various formulas and functions instead of applying that number directly to the formula. The value can be any length, but by giving it a name you simplify its use and cut down on errors by not typing the value incorrectly each time you enter it. It also makes updates easier as you only have to change the value in one place, not in each cell where it was used.

For example, you might have a "hardship multiplier" that you add to trainers' per diems when they are required to travel a particular distance, for a certain number of hours per day, or over a set number of days in a row. You might even have different hardship multipliers for each of those scenarios.

 What Microsoft Calls It: Define a constant

Step-by-Step

Create a Named Cell
In this example, a cell is named _15MinRate so it can be used in client billing formulas to calculate how much clients should be billed for the time a representative spent with them.

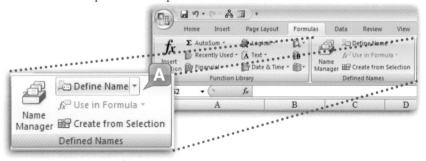

1. Select any empty cell, then click the **Define Name** button **A**. in the **Define Names** group of the **Formulas** tab to launch the **New Name** dialog box.

2. In the **Name** textbox **B** in the **New Name** dialog box, type a name for the value. The name you choose:

- Cannot contain spaces, punctuation, or symbols (except underscores).
- Cannot be the same as another name in the defined scope.

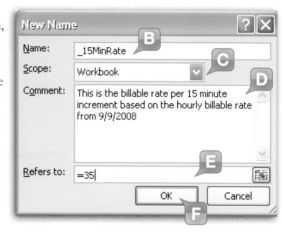

3. Select an option from the **Scope** dropdown menu **C**. The available options are for the name to apply to the whole workbook or to a single sheet.

4. In the **Comment** field **D**, provide a description about the named cell.

5. In the **Refers to** field **E**, enter the number your defined name needs to be.

6. Click the **OK** button **F**.

7. Use the named value in a formula **G**.

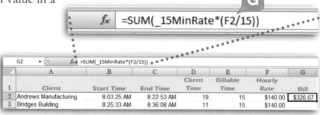

 Bright Idea: You can apply a name to a cell or a whole range of cells, rather than a single value. To do so, select the range of cells you want to name, and then follow the steps as if you were naming a value. The **Refers** to field will be pre-filled with your selected cells.

13 | Insert Subtotals

Difficulty: ●●○○

Subtotals are functions designed to apply various formulas to columns of data in order to facilitate review and analysis of the table's information.

Subtotals are dynamic in that they adjust instantly based on filters. This makes them very useful when you are reviewing a table as you can make small adjustments to see different perspectives on the information.

For example, if you are looking at a list of corporations that donated to your charitable cause throughout a year, the table might include the companies' total donations, dates of donations, industries, and location. You could insert a SUM subtotal at the bottom of the donations column and then review which industries were most supportive of your cause, which months saw the most donations or which counties were home to the biggest donors. This information might help you target your campaigns for the following year.

⌐ Step-by-Step

Create a Subtotal

1. Determine which column you want to subtotal by. In this example, the data in Column A will be used to subtotal the data .

	A	B	C	D	E	F
1	Item	Category	Store	Associate	Sale Price	Commission
2	Dishwasher	Appliance	1123	Andrews	$ 208.00	$166.40
3	Home Thtr	Audio	1123	Andrews	$ 501.00	$400.80
4	Refrigerator	Appliance	1123	Andrews	$5,904.00	$590.40
5	Stove	Appliance	1123	Andrews	$ 896.00	$716.80
6	Dishwasher	Appliance	1123	Cook	$1,027.00	$102.70
7	Home Thtr	Audio	1123	Cook	$ 200.00	$160.00
8	Refrigerator	Appliance	1123	Cook	$3,446.00	$344.60
9	Stove	Appliance	1123	Cook	$5,789.00	$578.90
10	Dishwasher	Appliance	1123	Flaherty	$ 500.00	$400.00
11	Home Thtr	Audio	1123	Flaherty	$5,007.00	$500.70
12	Refrigerator	Appliance	1123	Flaherty	$5,462.00	$546.20
13	Stove	Appliance	1123	Flaherty	$ 478.00	$382.40
14	Dishwasher	Appliance	1123	Frederickson	$ 375.00	$300.00
15	Home Thtr	Audio	1123	Frederickson	$2,374.00	$237.40
16	Refrigerator	Appliance	1123	Frederickson	$3,797.00	$379.70
17	Stove	Appliance	1123	Frederickson	$ 347.00	$277.60
18	Dishwasher	Appliance	1123	Jones	$ 654.00	$523.20
19	Home Thtr	Audio	1123	Jones	$2,004.00	$200.40
20	Refrigerator	Appliance	1123	Jones	$ 264.00	$211.20
21	Stove	Appliance	1123	Jones	$3,456.00	$345.60
22	Dishwasher	Appliance	1123	Sandler	$ 225.00	$180.00
23	Home Thtr	Audio	1123	Sandler	$ 690.00	$552.00
24	Refrigerator	Appliance	1123	Sandler	$4,754.00	$475.40
25	Stove	Appliance	1123	Sandler	$6,789.00	$678.90

2. Sort the selected column (Column A in this example) so that the like items in it are grouped **B**. This generates a subtotal for each item in the column.

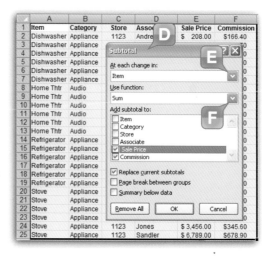

3. Click the **Subtotal** button **C** in the **Outline** group on the **Data** tab to launch the **Subtotal** dialog box **D**. This is where you make the selections that generate your subtotals.

4. Select the column you chose to subtotal by from the **At each change in** dropdown menu **E**. Column A is selected by default, and also happens to be Item, the one used in this example.

5. Select how you would like the data in your selected column subtotaled from the Use function dropdown menu **F**. The selected function is applied to the data in the column(s) you select from the **Add subtotal to** box. Some of the most common selections are:

- **Sum:** Adds the data in the selected column.

- **Count:** Counts and displays the number of rows that contain data in the selected column.

- **Average:** Computes an average from the data in the selected column.

- **Max and Min:** These selections identify the largest or smallest number in the selected column.

6. In the **Add subtotal to** box G, select the columns that will be subtotaled. The default selection is the final column (in this example Column F, Commission). This example also includes Column E, Sale Price.

7. Below the **Add subtotal to** box are additional options for subtotal layout. Click a checkbox H to select the associated option.

   - **Replace current subtotals:** Replaces any existing subtotals on the sheet with the ones you create here.

   - **Page break between groups:** Puts each subtotal on its own printed page.

   - **Summary below data:** Places the subtotals at the bottoms of each data group and places the grand total at the bottom of the data. If unchecked, the subtotals appear above the data groups and the grand total appears at the top of the data.

8. Click the **OK** button 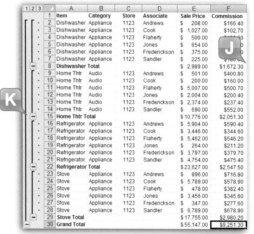 to generate your subtotals **J**.

9. Use the controls in the left margin **K** to expand or collapse the data for each group. You can also click the control next to grand total to collapse all data. 💡

Bright Idea: Once you have completed a subtotal, you can change the subtotal type. That way you can see the total sales and the average commission at the same time. To do so, select the cell that contains the subtotal you'd like to edit **L**. In the **Formula** bar, delete the **function_num** part of the **SUBTOTAL** function **M**. The deleted item is a number that corresponds to a function in the **function_num** dropdown **N**. In this formula it was nine before it was deleted. Then select a new numbered function from the dropdown.

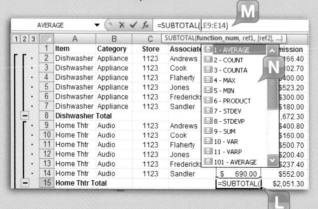

Once your constant is redefined, you can select a column that contains fields that include the "wrong" constant, press CTRL + H on your keyboard, and then find the old Fuction (9) and replace it with the new one (1).

14 | Insert a Basic Formula

Difficulty:

A formula in Excel is very similar to a formula in math. Writing an Excel formula is, in fact, exactly like writing a math problem, except that cell coordinates, or addresses, replace some numbers and variables.

Formulas are very useful for performing mathematical calculations between numbers and cells. For example, if you want to multiply a sales team's commission percentage by its sales totals, you can use a simple formula.

Once a formula is entered, the cell that contains it appears to only contain the result of the formula's calculation. Clicking on the cell reveals the formula behind the cell's value in the formula bar.

SEE ALSO: COPY A FORMULA TO MULTIPLE CELLS, APPENDIX C

	A	B	C	D	E
1	LastName	FirstName	$Q Sales	Comm %	Commision
2	Andrews	Angela	$ 2,751.00	6%	$ 165.06
3	Bridges	Serena	$ 3,552.00	4%	$ 142.08
4	Brown	Edna	$ 2,726.00	10%	$ 272.60
5	Cook	Rory	$ 5,041.00	12%	$ 604.92
6	Davis	Kim	$ 2,547.00	4%	$ 101.88
7	Douglas	James	$ 1,961.00	6%	$ 117.66
8	Flaherty	Andy	$ 3,275.00	6%	$ 196.50
9	Franklin	Jim	$ 2,486.00	4%	$ 99.44
10	Hawkins	Richard	$ 3,051.00	12%	$ 366.12
11	Johnson	Nicole	$ 3,462.00	10%	$ 346.20
12	Smith	Aiden	$ 1,618.00	6%	$ 97.08
13	Wilson	Erika	$ 1,442.00	4%	$ 57.68

Step-by-Step

Enter a Formula

1. Select the cell where you want the calculated total to appear **A**.

2. Click the formula bar **B** to place your cursor there.

	A	B	C	D	E
1	LastName	FirstName	3Q Sales	Comm %	Commision
2	Andrews	Angela	$ 2,751.00	6%	
3	Bridges	Serena	$ 3,552.00	4%	
4	Brown	Edna	$ 2,726.00	10%	
5	Cook	Rory	$ 5,041.00	12%	
6	Davis	Kim	$ 2,547.00	4%	
7	Douglas	James	$ 1,961.00	6%	
8	Flaherty	Andy	$ 3,275.00	6%	
9	Franklin	Jim	$ 2,486.00	4%	
10	Hawkins	Richard	$ 3,051.00	12%	
11	Johnson	Nicole	$ 3,462.00	10%	
12	Smith	Aiden	$ 1,618.00	6%	
13	Wilson	Erika	$ 1,442.00	4%	

3. Type = **C**.

	A	B	C	D	E
1	LastName	FirstName	3Q Sales	Comm %	Commision
2	Andrews	Angela	$ 2,751.00	6%	=
3	Bridges	Serena	$ 3,552.00	4%	
4	Brown	Edna	$ 2,726.00	10%	
5	Cook	Rory	$ 5,041.00	12%	

CONTINUE

4. Type the first value in your formula 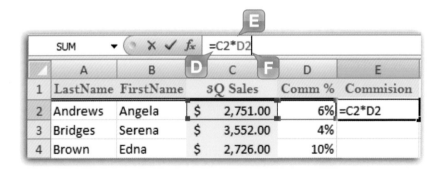 D whether that is a cell coordinate or a number.

5. Type an operator E between the two values in your formula.

Common Operators

+: This adds the two values.

-: This subtracts the second value from the first.

*: This multiplies the two values. (This is the operator used in this example.)

/: This divides the first value by the second.

^: Identifies a number as exponentiation.

6. Type the second value in the formula F.

7. Press the **ENTER** key on your keyboard to see the result .

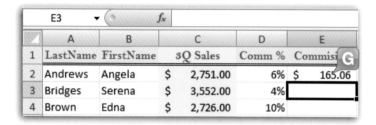

Bright Idea: You can create more complex formulas using additional math rules, such as parentheses to group various functions.

15 | Copy a Formula to Multiple Cells

Difficulty: ●●○○

You may want to use the same formula along an entire row or column of data, or even across several worksheets; for example, if you have a standard salary multiplier for overtime hours.

Instead of re-typing the formula each time you use it, you can simply copy it to multiple cells. As long as you are using "relative references" (coordinates without "$" markers in them), Excel will adjust the formula each time it copies to apply to associated data. For example, copying a formula that multiplies cell A1 by B1 to produce a value in C1 can be copied to C2 through C15, and Excel replaces A1 and B1 with A2 and B2 for row 2, and A3 and B3 for row 3, etc.

SEE ALSO: INSERT A BASIC FORMULA, INSERT A BASIC FUNCTION

Step-by-Step

Copy a Formula Using the Fill Handle

Use the **Fill Handle** to copy a formula to several adjacent cells.

1. Select the cell that contains the formula you want to copy **A**.

2. Hover your cursor around the black square in the lower right corner of the cell **B** until your cursor turns into a plus sign **C**.

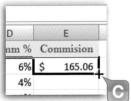

3. Click and hold the left mouse button while dragging the handle to include all cells where you would like the formula copied 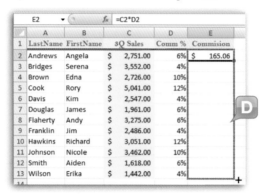.

4. Release the mouse button to populate the cells with the formula 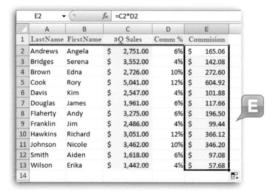.

Hot Tip: Copy the formula to non-adjacent cells by right-clicking the cell that contains the formula, select **Copy,** then right-click the destination cell and choose **Paste**.

Bright Idea: There may be times when you do not want Excel to adjust all or part of the formula for you. For example, if you have a table of standard multipliers that you use in the formula, you might want the same cell to always be used to multiply. You can create what is called an "absolute reference" by inserting a "$" sign to the left of the part of the cell coordinate that you want to stay the same. If you always want to use cell C2, you would write it as "C2".

STOP

16 | Calculate the Difference Between Two Times

Difficulty: ●○○○

There are times when the data you need to track or analyze is more complex than simple numbers. Equations that evaluate text, dates, and times all require special handling, and Excel has built-in tools ready to assist you with those evaluations.

For example, you might need to track how long a particular piece of equipment is used each day, or how long a bay door stays open during pickups and deliveries.

The actual calculations for times tend to be simple and straight-forward, but getting the data to display in a way that is useful and informative is often more challenging. ⚠

Step-by-Step

Calculate the Difference Between Two Times

In this example, the spreadsheet is used to calculate the number of minutes representatives spend talking to each client.

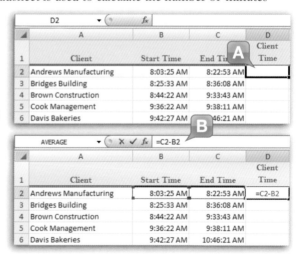

1. Select the cell where the result of the equation (the number of minutes) should appear **A**.

2. Type **=C2-B2** **B** to instruct Excel to subtract the Start Time data from the End Time data.

3. Press the **ENTER** key on your keyboard to complete the formula.

4. The result 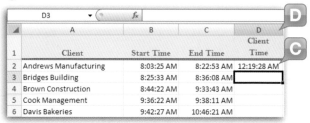 may not be what you expected or needed. Below, the result of the equation is displayed in the same HH:MM:SS (hours-minutes-seconds) format as the source cells. To change the appearance, change the formatting.

	A	B	C	D
				Client
1	Client	Start Time	End Time	Time
2	Andrews Manufacturing	8:03:25 AM	8:22:53 AM	12:19:28 AM
3	Bridges Building	8:25:33 AM	8:36:08 AM	
4	Brown Construction	8:44:22 AM	9:33:43 AM	
5	Cook Management	9:36:22 AM	9:38:11 AM	
6	Davis Bakeries	9:42:27 AM	10:46:21 AM	

5. Select **Column D**, Client Time 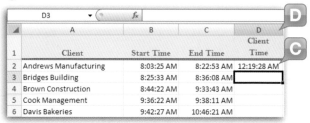.

6. Click the dialog box launcher for the **Number** group 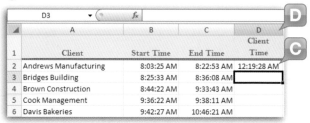 on the **Home** tab to launch the **Format Cells** dialog box.

7. On the **Number** tab, select **Custom** in the **Category** box 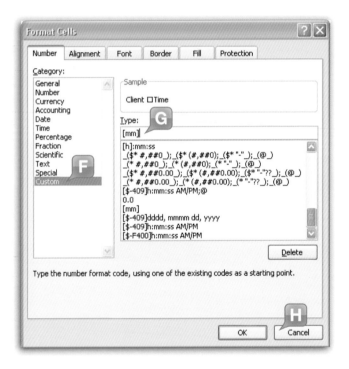.

8. In the **Type** text box, enter **[mm]** . This format tells Excel to display only the minutes.

9. Click the **OK** button .

10. Using the fill handle, drag the formula to the rest of the cells in the Client Time column and review your results .

	A	B	C	D
				Client
1	Client	Start Time	End Time	Time
2	Andrews Manufacturing	8:03:25 AM	8:22:53 AM	19
3	Bridges Building	8:25:33 AM	8:36:08 AM	10
4	Brown Construction	8:44:22 AM	9:33:43 AM	49
5	Cook Management	9:36:22 AM	9:38:11 AM	01
6	Davis Bakeries	9:42:27 AM	10:46:21 AM	63

E21 f_x

Caution: Excel automatically assumes any time you enter is AM unless you specify otherwise.

17 Count the Number of Work Days Between Two Dates

Difficulty:

Sometimes the data you are reviewing involves dates rather than just simple numbers.

For example, you might need to track how many days a particular project or process takes, or calculate the return on an investment based on how much time elapsed between a product's launch and when it generated enough revenue to cover its development.

Excel has a number of built-in date calculation functions to accomplish those tasks and many more. ⚠

⌐ Step-by-Step

Count the Number of Work Days Between Two Dates

In this example, a column is created to track the number of business days that elapse between the time an order is placed and when it ships.

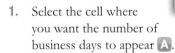

	A	B	C	D
1	Order #	Order_Date	Ship_Date	Fulfillment
2	1012	3/5/2007	3/9/2007	
3	1031	3/8/2007	3/15/2007	
4	1125	3/9/2007	3/15/2007	
5	1158	3/15/2007	3/19/2007	

D2   ▾   fx

1. Select the cell where you want the number of business days to appear A.

2. Type =**NETWORKDAYS** in the formula bar **B**. This function tells Excel to do two important things:

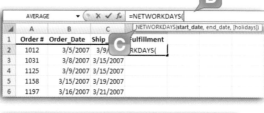

- Count both the start and end days of the date range as part of the total number of days tallied.

- Ignore any dates that fall on weekends.

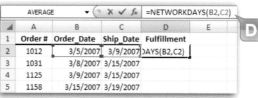

3. Follow the instructions in the **Formula Autocomplete** tooltip **C** to add **B2** as the **start_date** value and **C2** as the **end_date** value in the **NETWORKDAYS** formula **D**.

	A	B	C	D
1	Order #	Order_Date	Ship_Date	Fulfillment
2	1012	3/5/2007	3/9/2007	5
3	1031	3/8/2007	3/15/2007	6
4	1125	3/9/2007	3/15/2007	5
5	1158	3/15/2007	3/19/2007	3
6	1197	3/16/2007	3/21/2007	4
7	1258	3/18/2007	3/25/2007	5
8	1266	3/21/2007	3/27/2007	5
9	1268	3/24/2007	3/31/2007	5
10	1315	3/25/2007	4/5/2007	9
11	1402	3/31/2007	4/10/2007	7

4. Press the **ENTER** key on your keyboard to complete the formula.

5. Use the fill handle to drag the formula to the other cells in the Fulfillment column **E**.

 Caution: Be sure you assign a date format to the column where you have dates. Excel's default date format is a number.

 Hot Tip: Exclude holidays by adding a comma after the end_date value and entering cell addresses that contain dates your company is closed. For example, =NETWORKDAYS(A2,B2,C2:E2) would count the number of Monday through Friday days between the dates specified in A2 and B2, less the holiday dates in C2, D2, and E2.

STOP

18

Insert a Basic Function

Difficulty: ●●●○

Functions are different from Formulas in that they are often combinations of different formulas that have been named and can be used by name to accomplish advanced calculations with ease.

Using functions is often even easier than using formulas. Excel recognizes when you are using a function and prompts you with correct terminology and formatting to make using them a breeze. A built-in feature called the "Function Wizard" even helps you decide which function you need to achieve the results you are looking for.

Functions are useful because they allow you to quickly apply mathematical, logical, financial, and text-based formulas to your data. For example, you might bill clients by the quarter hour, rather than by minutes. In that case, you would want to take raw time data and round it to the nearest quarter hour to determine how much a client owes you. A function will allow you to do that with just a few clicks.

Step-by-Step

Insert a Function

This example uses the **ROUNDUP** function to round up from a decimal. The company wants to order supplies in even increments of 100 items. To accomplish this, the Total Needed will need to be rounded up to the nearest 100 items above the required total. In other words, if 1447 items are needed, 1500 should be ordered.

1. Select the cell where you want your rounded-up result to appear .

	A	B	C	D	E	F
1	Items	Beaumont	Regency	Edwardsville	Needed	Ordered
2	Calendars	239	646	562	1447	
3	Handbooks	256	498	664	1418	
4	Ledgers	47	89	893	1029	
5	Planners	172	88	1087	1347	

F2   *fx*

2. Type **=ROUND** in the formula bar **B**.

3. Double-click the **ROUNDUP** option in the **Formula Autocomplete** menu **C**.

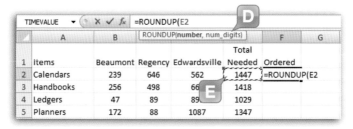

4. The **Formula Autocomplete** tooltip **D** shows you what information is required to complete the **ROUNDUP** function—the number to be rounded (number) and the number of decimal places to which that number should be rounded (num_digits).

5. The number in cell E2 (**1447**) is the one that will be rounded up. Click cell E2 **E** to select it.

6. Type a comma **G** to separate the number to be rounded from the number of digits it should be rounded to.

7. Type the number of digits to which the final result should be rounded. In this example, **-2** was selected **H**.

G **H**

AVERAGE	▼	X ✓ *fx*	=ROUNDUP(E2,-2)		

	A	B	C	D	E	F
					Total	
1	Items	Beaumont	Regency	Edwardsville	Neded	Ordered
2	Calendars	239	646	562	1447	=ROUND
3	Handbooks	256	498	664	1418	
4	Ledgers	47	89	893	1029	
5	Planners	172	88	1087	1347	

- If you select a positive number, such as 1, 2, or 3, a decimal point is added to the end of the number, and the number is rounded up to the number of decimal places, tenths, hundredths, thousandths, you selected **I**.

- If you select 0, the number rounds up to the nearest whole number **J**.

- If you enter a negative number, such as -1, -2, or -3, the numbers to the left of the decimal place are replaced with zeroes to the number of digits (tens, hundreds, thousands) you selected **K**.

A	B	C	
Rounded Number	Formula	Result	
1447.6789	=ROUNDUP(A2,3)	1447.679	**I**
1447.6789	=ROUNDUP(A3,2)	1447.68	
1447.6789	=ROUNDUP(A4,1)	1447.7	
1447.6789	=ROUNDUP(A5,0)	1448	**J**
1447.6789	=ROUNDUP(A6,-1)	1450	
1447.6789	=ROUNDUP(A7,-2)	1500	**K**
1447.6789	=ROUNDUP(A8,-3)	2000	

8. Press the **ENTER** key on your keyboard to see the result.

9. Copy the formula to the rest of the cells in the column L using the fill handle.

	A	B	C	D	E	F
					Total	
1	Items	Beaumont	Regency	Edwardsville	Needed	Ordered
2	Calendars	239	646	562	1447	1500
3	Handbooks	256	498	664	1418	1500
4	Ledgers	47	89	893	1029	1100
5	Planners	172	88	1087	1347	1400

19 | Use Conditional Functions

Difficulty:

Most of the time the formulas and functions you use in your worksheet will be designed to yield a single result. You want to add, subtract, multiply, or divide various sheet data; check for duplicates; or search for particular zip codes. Sometimes, though, you need a formula that changes depending on the data in the cell.

Conditional functions and formulas make formatting those logical decisions easy. The conditional functions typically contain "if" in their names. IF, SUMIF, and COUNTIF are the most commonly used options.

For example, if you have a list of employees, you may want to know how many receive company benefits. If you have a column that contains that data, you can create a COUNTIF formula in another cell to check the benefits column for a Y or an N and count the ones that contain a Y.

Alternately, you may create a list of customers and need to know how many have not yet paid their bill this month and the amount of outstanding revenue. You can create fields that count the number of customers who have "$0.00" in their monthly payment column, and apply a SUMIF formula on the monthly payments due column contingent on "$0.00" being in the monthly payment column.

	A	B	C	D	E	F
1	LastName	FirstName	Benefits	Hire_Date	Salary	Dept
2	Brown	Angela	Y	6/3/2003	$ 47,000.00	Acctg.
3	Douglas	Serena	Y	1/25/2009	$ 52,000.00	IT
4	Franklin	Edna	N	8/7/2004	$ 33,000.00	Sales
5	Hawkins	Rory	Y	9/16/2004	$ 22,000.00	Admin.
6	Johnson	Kim	N	1/2/2005	$ 57,000.00	Acctg.
7	Smith	James	N	8/20/2007	$ 35,000.00	Mktg.
8	Wilson	Andy	Y	12/8/2008	$ 67,000.00	H.R.
9						
10	Empoyees w/ Benefits:		4			

SEE ALSO: APPENDIX C

	A	B	C	D	E
1	Due_Date	Customer	Due	Pmts	Total February Outstanding
2	1/15/2008	Able	$ 365.00	$365.00	$2,278.00
3	1/15/2008	Agnew	$ 778.00	$1,000.00	
4	1/15/2008	Anderson	$ 1,029.00	$0.00	
5	1/15/2008	Crew	$ 124.00	$150.00	
6	1/15/2008	Crew	$ 124.00	$0.00	
7	1/15/2008	Dandy	$ 1,125.00	$0.00	
8	1/15/2008	Dunston	$ 875.00	$900.00	
9	1/15/2008	Dunston	$ 875.00	$875.00	

Step-by-Step

Use Conditional Functions

In this example, **Column E** (Pmt_Status) is created where **Column D** (Pmts) is evaluated against **Column C** (Due) to determine if the account is current or delinquent. If the payments are greater than or equal to the amount due, the account will be marked "Current," but if the payments are less than the amount due, the account is marked "Delinquent."

1. Select the cell where you want the conditional formula to appear **A**.

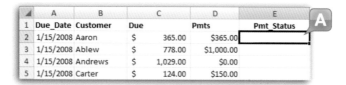

2. Type =**IF** to start the function **B**.

3. Double-click the **IF** option in the **Formula Autocomplete** dropdown that appears **C**.

CONTINUE

4. The **Formula Autocomplete** tooltip 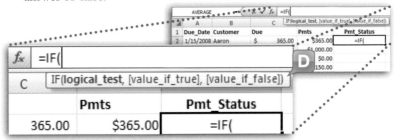 shows you exactly what you need to enter to successfully complete the function.

- **logical_test:** This is the equation that evaluates if the condition is true or false.

- **value_if_true:** This is what the cell contains if the logical test yields an answer of true.

- **value_if_false:** This is what the cell contains if the logical test yields an answer of false.

5. Considering the payments are being evaluated to determine if they are greater than or equal to the amount due, the **logical_test** is **D:D>=C:C** 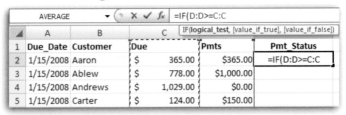. D:D tells Excel to measure each item in column D. The operators > and = describe which measurement will be done. C:C tells Excel what D:D should be compared to.

- **>:** The number on the left side of the symbol is greater than the one on the right. 8>7

- **<:** The number on the left side of the symbol is lesser than the one on the right. 7<8.

- **>=:** The number on the left side of the symbol is greater than or equal to the one on the right. 7>=7, 8>=7.

- **<=:** The number on the left side of the symbol is lesser than or equal to the one on the right. 7<=8, 8<=8.

6. The **value_if_true** text displays if the amount in **Column D** (Pmts), is greater than or equal to what is in **Column C** (Due) is **"Current"** F. For Excel to understand that it should insert the value as text, it must be enclosed in quotation marks.

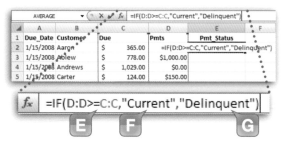

7. The **value_if_false** text displays if the amount in **Column D**, (Pmts), is less than the amount in **Column C** (Due) is **"Delinquent"** G.

8. Type **)** to complete the function.

9. Press the **ENTER** key on your keyboard.

10. Verify that the first cell displays the appropriate result, then drag it over a few more cells to test. When you are confident it is working correctly, drag it to the entire column H.

STOP

20 | Troubleshoot Formula and Function Errors

Difficulty: ●●○○

Sometimes your data may not look correct, or you may get an error but not know exactly where the problem is. Excel includes a simple tool to check for and fix errors.

Formulas can become quite complex over time, especially when worksheets have multiple formulas that use one-another to produce various results, subtotals, totals, and reports.

What Microsoft Calls It: Check for errors

Step-by-Step

Perform Error Checking on Formulas

1. You have an error in your calculations when you see the error marker and/or the text **#VALUE!** in a cell .

2. Click the **Error Checking** button 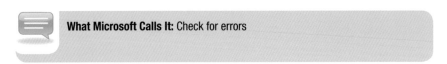 in the **Formula Auditing** group of the **Formulas** tab to launch the **Error Checking** dialog box.

3. If there are errors in your formula, the dialog box lists them 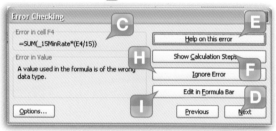, and explains the problem below. Click through the errors found using the **Previous** and **Next** buttons D.

4. For each error, choose one or more actions:

- Click the **Help on This Error** button E to review the Excel Help text on the error.

- Click the **Show Calculation Steps** button F to view the formula with all source data in place G.

- Click the **Ignore Error** button H to take no corrective action on any given error.

- Click the **Edit in Formula Bar** button I to edit the calculation in the formula bar.

5. Once you have viewed and taken action on each error found during the error check, click the **OK** button J in the confirmation dialog box to conclude the check.

Find Formulas, Functions, and Cells Connected to a Cell

Difficulty:

There may be times when you look at a workbook and need to know which cells are tied to one-another using formulas and functions.

You may be working on a worksheet that others have used, or inherited a worksheet that someone else set up. You may have added so many formulas and functions to the workbook that you can't remember where all of the relationships are. You also may experience errors that will require you to investigate which other information might be effected.

For example, in a spreadsheet you are working on, cell A2 contains a value that is used in a formula in cell B2. Because B2 **depends** on cell A2 to calculate its value, it is a **dependent** of cell A2. Because a value must be in cell A2 **before** a value can be calculated in cell B2, cell A2 is a **precedent** of cell B2.

Excel offers a simple way to review which cells are both dependent on and depended upon by other cells.

 What Microsoft Calls It: Trace precedents and dependents

 *Step-by-Step*

Find Formulas, Functions, and Cells Connected to a Cell

1. Open your workbook to a sheet you know contains cells that have either precedents or dependents. 🔥

2. Select the cell in which you want to check precedents and/or dependents.

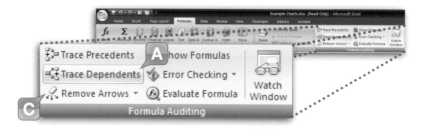

3. Click the **Trace Precedents** or **Trace Dependents** button 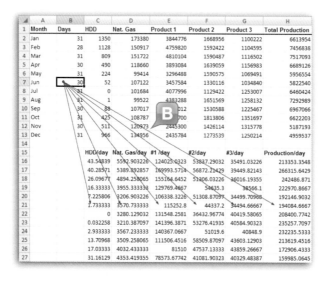 A in the **Formula Auditing** group of the **Formulas** tab. In this example the dependents for cell B7 are checked.

4. Arrows leading from the selected cell extend and point to those cells that use its data in their calculations B.

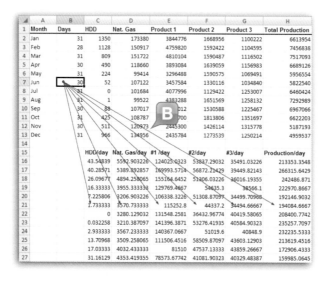

Hot Tip: Click the **Remove Arrows** button C to clear all precedent and dependent arrows from the screen.

22 | Calculate Percentages in a PivotTable

Difficulty:

PivotTables do a wonderful job of revealing the important information hidden in your data. Part of what makes them so useful is their flexibility. They can show you your information from a variety of perspectives with just a few mouse clicks.

Once you have your data arranged in a PivotTable, you can adjust how you view the information you are analyzing. One way you can adjust the data picture your PivotTable presents is to display numbers and figures as percentages rather than subtotals or grand totals.

For example, looking at revenue totals by sales rep shows you your top performers. However, looking at those same numbers as percentages gives you an idea of who is not only producing, but contributing what percentage of your total revenue to the bottom line. This is valuable when you want to calculate bonuses, to help prepare for reviews or quarterly reports, or when determining good matchups for mentoring new or under-performing team members.

Making this adjustment is very easy and provides you a great deal about the business or processes your data is measuring.

SEE ALSO: CREATE A PIVOTTABLE

⌐ Step-by-Step

Calculate Percentages in a PivotTable

1. Click on any field in your PivotTable.

2. In the **Choose fields to add to report** selection box of the **PivotTable Field List** panel, click the field **A** for which you want to calculate percentages.

3. In the **Active Field** group on the **Options** tab of the highlighted **PivotTables** section, click the **Field Settings** button **B** to launch the **Value Field Settings** dialog box.

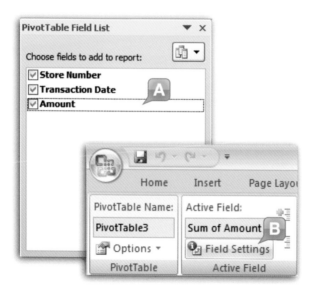

4. In the **Value Field Settings** dialog box, click the **Show values as** tab and select the percentage option that matches your needs from the **Show values as** dropdown menu **C**. Common selections include:

    *   **Difference From:** This calculation displays each cell's value as a difference between itself and a number you select.

    *   **% of:** This calculation displays each cell's value as a percentage of a number you select.

    *   **% of total:** This calculation displays each cell's value as a percentage of the range's total.

    *   **% of row:** This calculation displays each cell's value as a percentage of its row.

    *   **% of column:** This calculation displays each cell's value as a percentage of its column.

5. Click the **Number Format** button **D** to launch the **Format Cells** dialog box.

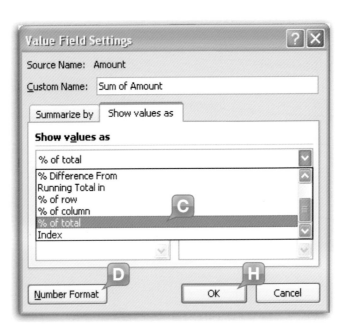

6. In the **Format Cells** dialog box, select **Percentage** 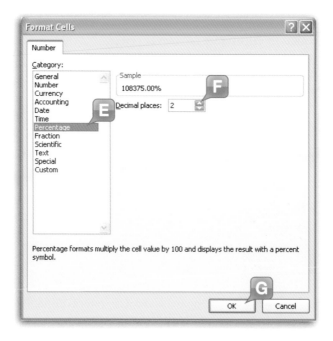 from the **Category** selection box and then use the **Decimal Places** control to set the number of decimal places you want your percentage to include.

7. Click the **OK** button in the **Format Cells** dialog box.

8. Click the **OK** button in the **Value Field Settings** dialog box.

23 Create a PivotTable Calculated Field

Difficulty: ●●●○

PivotTables are powerful by themselves, but they can become more powerful yet by adding additional features and functions. Calculated Fields and Calculated Items are two additions that can reveal more about your data than could the PivotTable alone.

When you want to create a new PivotTable field that uses existing PivotTable fields in a formula or calculation, you need to create a calculated field.

For example, your charitable organization donates money to provide assistance to families each month. You have a PivotTable that contains fields which tell you both how many families you helped each month and how much money was donated to families each month. It might be helpful for you to determine how much money was given to each family. A calculated field that divides the monthly dollars donated by the number of families helped monthly would tell you that.

SEE ALSO: CREATE A PIVOTTABLE

Step-by-Step

Create a PivotTable Calculated Field

The field created in this example subtracts the daily returns from the daily sales for each of a retailer's stores.

1. Click on any field in the PivotTable.

2. Click the **Formulas** button in the **Tools** group of the **Options** tab in the highlighted **PivotTable Tools** section of the ribbon.

3. Select **Calculated Field** B from the **Formulas** dropdown button.

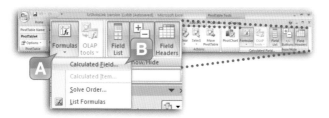

4. In the **Insert Calculated Field** dialog box, type a descriptive name for your field in the **Name** textbox C.

5. In the **Formula** textbox, replace the initial "0" with the fields and operators you want to use in your calculation. In this example, we have added Sales, a "minus sign" and Returns D to show we are subtracting one from the other.

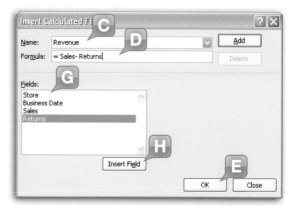

6. Click the **OK** button E.

7. Review your new field and data F. Note that changes and additions were made to several areas of the PivotTable.

Hot Tip: Either type a field name in the **Formula** textbox, or select the field in the **Fields** box G and then click the **Insert Field** button H.

STOP

24 Create a PivotTable Calculated Item

Difficulty:

PivotTables are great for organizing your data and displaying it in a very accessible and comprehensible way. Sometimes, though, you may want to add additional components to them to show tabulated data.

Create a calculated item to create a new item or category in an existing PivotTable field using other items or categories from that same field in a formula or calculation.

For example, you might have a field in a PivotTable that contains a list of your organization's volunteers by skill—carpentry, graphic design, grant writing, electrician, clerical, plumber, and so forth. As you plan the next year's budget, recruiting efforts, and projects, it might be helpful to know the total of each kind of volunteer you have—laborers versus office workers. A Calculated Item allows you to obtain that information.

SEE ALSO: INSERT A PIVOTTABLE

Step-by-Step

Create a PivotTable Calculated Item

In this example, the higher-priced items sold by a store are being grouped into a new category called "Big Ticket" to isolate how much revenue those larger purchases bring in.

1. Select an item in your PivotTable **A**.

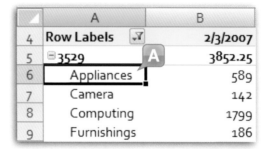

2. Click the **Formulas** button **B** in the **Tools** group of the **Options** tab in the highlighted **PivotTable Tools** section of the ribbon.

3. Click the **Calculated Item** option **C** from the **Formulas** dropdown button selections.

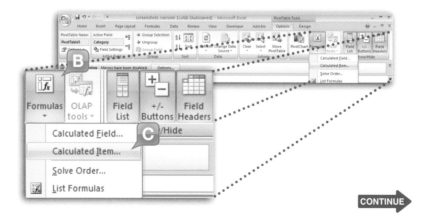

CONTINUE

4. In the **Insert Calculated Item** dialog box, type a descriptive name for your item in the **Name** textbox D.

5. In the **Formula** textbox E, replace the initial "0" with the fields and operators you want to use in the calculation. In this example, we have selected **Appliances**, **LgElec**, **Furnishings** and **Computing**, all separated by "plus signs," to show we are adding those fields together. 🔥

6. Click the **Add** button I.

7. Click the **OK** button J.

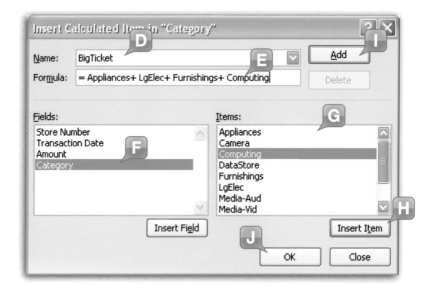

8. Review your new item **K**.

	A	B
4	**Row Labels** 🔽	2/3/2007
5	⊟ 3529	7201.25
6	Appliances	589
7	Camera	142
8	Computing	1799
9	Furnishings	186
10	LgElec	775
11	Media-Vid	89.25
12	SmElect **K**	272
13	BigTicket	3349

Hot Tip: You can either type a field name in the **Formula** textbox, or you can select the field in the **Fields** box **F**. Double-click an item from the **Items** box **G** (or click the **Insert Item** button **H**) to insert it.

25 Use Data Filters

Difficulty: ⬤⬤◯◯

Many Excel spreadsheets contain more data than one person needs to review at a given time. There are a number of tools that allow you to isolate specific pieces of information for examination, but one of the fastest methods is through filtering.

For example, if you are looking at a list of sales records for a particular time period (a day, a week, a month, etc.), you might want to examine all but one sales associate, one product, or one store. Filtering allows you to do that quickly and easily.

Step-by-Step

Apply a Data Filter to Your Sheet

1. Click any cell **A** in the data group you want to filter.

2. Choose to Filter your data. ✓

	A	B	C	D	E
1	Item	Category	Store	Associate	Sale Price
2	Dishwasher	Appliances	1123	Andrews	$ 208.00
3	Refrigerator	Appliances	1123	Andrews	$ 998.00
4	Refrigerator	Appliances	1123	Andrews	$ 1,027.00
5	Stereo	Audio	1123	Andrews	$ 119.00
6	BluRay	Video	1123	Andrews	$ 399.00
7	Stove	Appliances	2354	Bridges	$ 540.00
8	Stove	Appliances	2354	Bridges	$ 798.00
9	Refrigerator	Appliances	2354	Bridges	$ 1,328.00
10	Home Thtr	Audio	2354	Bridges	$ 652.00
11	BluRay	Video	2354	Bridges	$ 234.00
12	Speaker	Audio	3543	Brown	$ 78.00
13	LCDTV	Video	3543	Brown	$ 450.00
14	LCDTV	Video	3543	Brown	$ 798.00
15	LCTV	Video	3543	Brown	$ 1,400.00
16	Stove	Appliances	1123	Cook	$ 623.00
17	Refrigerator	Appliances	1123	Cook	$ 873.00
18	Refrigerator	Appliances	1123	Cook	$ 1,132.00
19	Stereo	Audio	1123	Cook	$ 398.00

3. Click the dropdown arrows 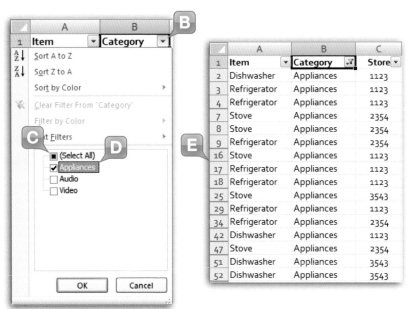 **B** that appear at the top of each column to reveal filtering choices for that column of data.

4. Uncheck the **Select All** box **C** and check the box(es) for the items you want to isolate. In this example **Appliances** **D** was selected in **Column B**, Category.

5. Review your selection **E**.

Option:
- On the **Home** tab, click the **Sort & Filter** button **F** in the **Editing** group.
- On the **Data** tab, click the **Filter** button **G** in the **Sort & Filter** group.

26 | Highlight Cells Based on Specific Criteria

Difficulty:

Sometimes the amount of data to look at on a given sheet is overwhelming. What you really want is a quick "big picture" view of your sheet so you know where you stand. Conditional formatting can do that for you.

	A	B	C
1		3Q Target	3Q To Date
2	Andrews	$10,000.00	$ 9,763.00
3	Bridges	$13,000.00	$ 7,884.00
4	Cook	$ 5,000.00	$ 5,102.00
5	Davis	$ 1,500.00	$ 700.00
6	Flaherty	$25,000.00	$ 37,884.00

Conditional formatting means that the formatting applied to the cells changes dynamically based on conditions. It is used to make at-a-glance spreadsheet and data analysis possible.

If you are tracking sales revenue by sales associate, you might choose a three color scale that highlights your lowest sales numbers in red, your highest in green, and the middle numbers in yellow.

	A	B	C
1		3Q Target	3Q To Date
2	Andrews	$10,000.00	$ 9,763.00
3	Bridges	$13,000.00	$ 7,884.00
4	Cook	$ 5,000.00	$ 5,102.00
5	Davis	$ 1,500.00	$ 700.00
6	Flaherty	$25,000.00	$ 37,884.00

Conditional formatting can be based on pre-set rules available via the **Conditional Formatting** dropdown menu, can be customized using Data Bars, Color Scales and Icon sets, or can be customized based on rules you create "from scratch."

 What Microsoft Calls It: Conditional Formatting

Step-by-Step

Format a Worksheet Based on Pre-Set Rules

Use this method to quickly apply a conditional format to a selection of cells with numeric data.

1. Select the cells to which you want to apply conditional formatting .

2. Click the **Conditional Formatting** button in the **Styles** group on the **Home** tab to open the **Conditional Formatting** menu.

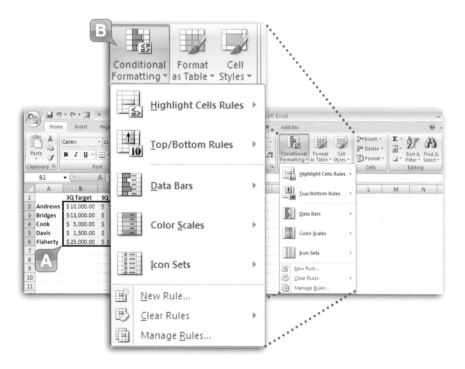

CONTINUE

Highlight Cells Based on Specific Criteria   **73**

3. Select one of the **Rules** options 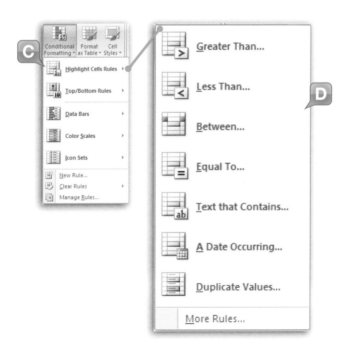.

Highlight Cell Rules D

- **Greater Than/Less Than**: Cells whose values are greater or less than a value you choose are highlighted.

- **Between**: Cells whose values are between two numbers you choose are highlighted.

- **Equal To**: Cells whose values are equal to a number you choose are highlighted.

- **Text that Contains**: Cells that contain text you choose are highlighted.

- **A Date Occurring**: Cells that contain dates matching your criteria are highlighted.

- **Duplicate Values**: Cells that contain values identical to one-another are highlighted.

Top/Bottom Rules

- **Top Ten/Bottom Ten Items**: Highlights the highest ten or lowest ten values.

- **Top 10%/Bottom 10%**: Highlights the cells that contain values that fall into the highest or lowest 10% of those in your selection.

- **Above or Below Average**: Establishes an average for your sheet and highlights cells that contain values above or below that average number.

4. In the specialized dialog box that appears for your selected rule, specify any additional criteria and select the formatting that applies to the relevant cells.

5. Click the **OK** button.

27 | Use Graphics to Compare Cell Values

Difficulty:

When you review large quantities of data, it can be very helpful to apply at-a-glance formatting options that make it easy to find the information you are looking for.

Excel provides several options for graphic and color format that make reviewing your sheet fast and easy.

  What Microsoft Calls It: Conditional Formatting

Step-by-Step

Using Data Bars, Color Scales, and Icon Sets

Use this method to highlight cells in a way that provides at-a-glance value comparison between all selected cells.

1. Select the cells to apply conditional formatting.

2. Click the **Conditional Formatting** button in the **Styles** group on the **Home** tab to open the **Conditional Formatting** menu.

3. Select one of the **Rules** options.

    *   **Data Bars:** A Shades cells with a gradient based on ther comparative values (higher numbers have longer bars).

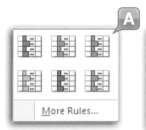

- **Color Scales:** B Shades cells with colors based on their comparative values (one color for low values, one for high, and—optionally—one for mid-range).

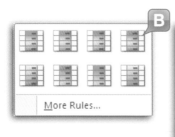

	A	B	C
1		3Q Target	3Q To Date
2	Andrews	$10,000.00	$ 9,763.00
3	Bridges	$13,000.00	$ 7,884.00
4	Cook	$ 5,000.00	$ 5,102.00
5	Davis	$ 1,500.00	$ 700.00
6	Flaherty	$25,000.00	$ 37,884.00

- **Icon Sets:** C Adds an icon to cells based on their comparative values by as many as five measurements.

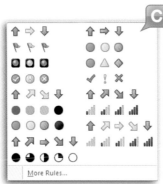

	A	B	C
1		3Q Target	3Q To Date
2	Andrews	$10,000.00	$ 9,763.00
3	Bridges	$13,000.00	$ 7,884.00
4	Cook	$ 5,000.00	$ 5,102.00
5	Davis	$ 1,500.00	$ 700.00
6	Flaherty	$25,000.00	$37,884.00

4. In the specialized dialog box that appears for your selected rule, specify any additional criteria and select the formatting to apply to the relevant cells.

CONTINUE

Use Graphics to Compare Cell Values   77

Step-by-Step

Create Custom Rules From Scratch

Use this method when none of the pre-set rules and formats meet your conditional formatting needs.

1. Select the cells to which you want to apply conditional formatting.

2. Open the **New Formatting Rule** dialog box **A**.

   • Select **New Rule** from the **Conditional Formatting** dropdown box **B** in the **Styles** group on the **Home** tab.

   • Choose the **More Rules** option **C** from the bottom of any of the other conditional formatting menus.

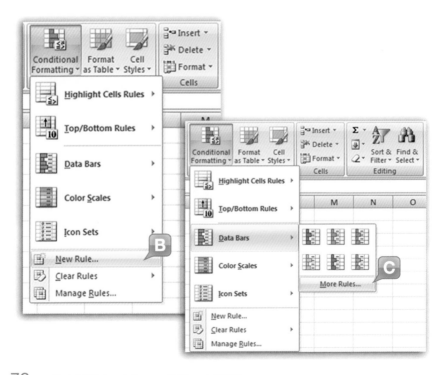

3. Select the type of rule to use as a template from the **Select a Rule Type** pane 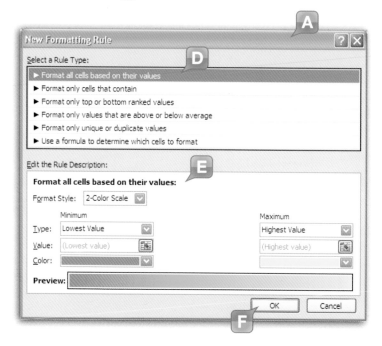.

4. Adjust the rules and formatting options that appear in the **Edit the Rule Description** pane **E**.

5. Click the **OK** button **F**.

28 | Create a PivotTable

Difficulty: ●●●○

PivotTables are among the most powerful data analysis tools available today—and also some of the most under-used.

PivotTables allow you to take static, dull spreadsheet data and give it meaning by allowing it to answer specific questions. For example, if you have a table that tracks customer sales data, your spreadsheet might include the customer's name, payment method, how much was spent, when purchases were made, and what kinds of items were purchased.

PivotTables can show at a glance what items or item categories are most popular, what methods of payment are used to purchase which items, and the days the store sees the highest sales. The store can target credit card customers with specific incentives, time coupon releases to coordinate with the days that are high-volume, or offer buy-one-get-one promotions that pair the items needed to sell more of with those that already perform well.

SEE ALSO: DELETE A PIVOTTABLE, CHANGE HOW DATA IS DISPLAYED IN A PIVOTTABLE, GROUP DATA WITHIN A PIVOTTABLE, CREATE A PIVOTTABLE CALCULATED FIELD, CREATE A PIVOTTABLE CALCULATED ITEM, CREATE A CHART FROM YOUR PIVOTTABLE

Customer	Pmt	Price	Coupon	Item	Category	Prch Date	WkDay
Smith	Cash	213.54	0	Stereo	Audio	3/3/2007	Saturday
Jones	Cash	83.06	0	Cell Phone	Mobile	3/3/2007	Saturday
Wilson	Credit	14.37	0	CD	Media	3/3/2007	Saturday
Edmonds	Credit	55.92	1	DVD BxSet	Media	3/3/2007	Saturday
Garr	Credit	1832.28	1	PL TV 62"	Video	3/4/2007	Sunday
Charles	Debit	22.08	1	Pwr Strip	Accessory	3/4/2007	Sunday
Deaton	Debit	96.08	0	Extension	Warranties	3/4/2007	Sunday
Rogers	Cash	224.93	1	Zune 80	Audio	3/4/2007	Sunday
Elis	Check	331.62	1	Blu Ray P	Video	3/4/2007	Sunday
Katz	Check	69.85	1	17" LT Bag	Accessory	3/4/2007	Sunday

Sum of Coupon	Column Labels ▼		
Row Labels ▼	Sunday	Saturday	Grand Total
⊟ 17" LT Bag	1		1
Accessory	1		1
⊟ Blu Ray P	1		1
Video	1		1
⊟ CD		0	0
Media		0	0
⊟ Cell Phone		0	0
Mobile		0	0
⊟ DVD BxSet		1	1
Media		1	1
⊟ Extension	0		0
Warranties	0		0
⊟ PL TV 62"	1		1
Video	1		1
⊟ Pwr Strip	1		1
Accessory	1		1
⊟ Stereo		0	0
Audio		0	0
⊟ Zune 80	1		1
Audio	1		1
Grand Total	**5**	**1**	**6**

Step-by-Step

Create a PivotTable

1. Select the data to include in your PivotTable, including column headers.

2. Click on the **Insert** tab and select **PivotTable** from the **Tables** panel to open the **Create PivotTable** dialog .

3. Select:
   - Data you want to analyze (the default is your selected cells).
   - Where to place the PivotTable.

If you choose to place it on your current sheet you need to select the cells where you'd like it to sit.

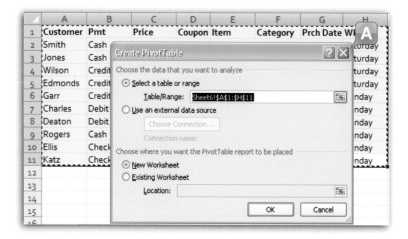

CONTINUE

4. Click the **OK** button 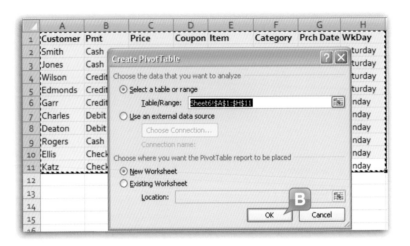 **B**. This opens the **PivotTable Field List** pane **C** and makes the **PivotTable Tools** tabs **D** available for use.

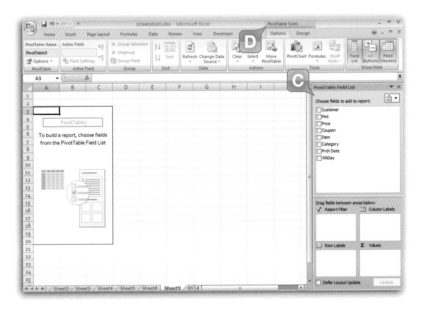

5. In the **Choose fields to add to report** window 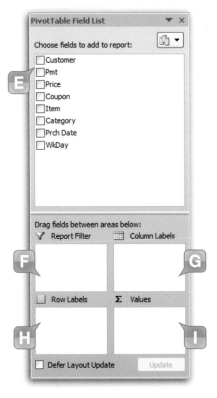 of the **PivotTable Field** List panel, check the fields to include in the PivotTable.

6. Click and drag fields to display in the following boxes:
   - **Report Filter box**: Fields dragged into this box control what data is filtered on in the PivotTable **F**.
   - **Column Labels**: Fields dragged here will be displayed as columns **G**.
   - **Row Labels**: Fields dragged here will be displayed as rows **H**.
   - **∑ Values**: Fields dragged here will display as data **I**.

Bright Idea: Change the items included in the PivotTable. Click any cell in the PivotTable and make your adjustments when the **PivotTable Field List** panel reappears.

29 | Delete a PivotTable

Difficulty: ●○○○

There are times when you do not want to edit a PivotTable, but want to completely delete it.

 **Step-by-Step**

Delete a PivotTable

1. Click anywhere in the PivotTable to be deleted.

2. In the highlighted **PivotTable Tools** section **A**, click the **Options** tab **B** .

3. In the **Actions** panel **C**, click the **Select** button **D**.

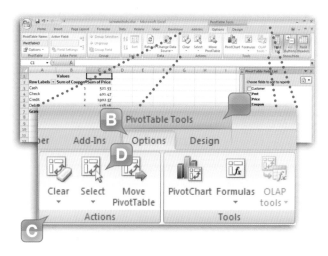

4. On the context menu that appears, choose **Entire PivotTable** 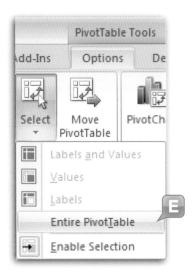.

5. Press the **DELETE** key on your keyboard.

Hot Tip: When the data behind a PivotTable is updated or changed you don't need to delete your table and re-create it to reflect the new data. Instead, refresh the table to show the new information. To do so, click on any cell in the PivotTable to reveal the **PivotTable Tools** segment of the Ribbon. On the **Options** tab, click the **Refresh** button in the **Data** group.

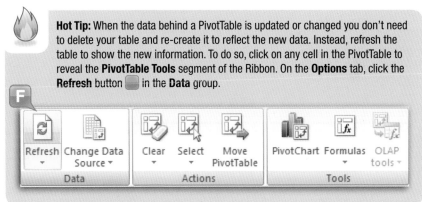

30 | Change How Data is Displayed in a PivotTable

Difficulty: ●●●●

Sometimes you may want to change the way that data is displayed in your PivotTable. The default data display format in a PivotTable is "Count." This means that for each category selected, the PivotTable shows whether or not there is a value in each associated cell.

For example, in the table at right, the number of coupons used in any given transaction is listed in the Coupon column . A "0" indicates no coupon was used, though it is a value in the cell (the cell is not empty). As a result, the default settings for a PivotTable would show that coupons were used in every transaction **B** (because the default of Count indicates a value—any value—is present in the cell).

	A	B	C	D	E	F
1	Customer	Pmt	Price	Coupon	Item	Category
2	Smith	Cash	213.54	0	Stereo	Audio
3	Jones	Cash	83.06	0	Cell Phone	Mobile
4	Wilson	Credit	14.37	0	CD	Media
5	Edmonds	Credit	55.92	1	DVD BxSet	Media
6	Garr	Credit	1832.28	1	PL TV 62"	Video
7	Charles	Debit	22.08	1	Pwr Strip	Accessory
8	Deaton	Debit	96.08	0	Extension	Warranties
9	Rogers	Cash	224.93	1	Zune 80	Audio
10	Ellis	Check	331.62	1	Blu Ray P	Video
11	Katz	Check	69.85	1	17" LT Bag	Accessory

	A	B	C
1		Values	
2	Row Labels ▾	Count of Coupon S	Price
3	Cash	3	521.53
4	Check	2	401.47
5	Credit	3	1902.57
6	Debit	2	118.16
7	**Grand Total**	10	2943.73

If you change the default for that data display from Count to Sum, you get a much more accurate picture of what is going on **C**.

	A	B	C
1		Values	
2	Row Labels ▾	Sum of Coupon S	Price
3	Cash	1	521.53
4	Check	2	401.47
5	Credit	2	1902.57
6	Debit	1	118.16
7	**Grand Total**	6	2943.73

What Microsoft Calls It: Summarize Data By

Change How PivotTable Data is Displayed

1. Right-click any cell in a column where you would like to change the way data is displayed.

2. In the context menu that appears, click **Summarize Data By** 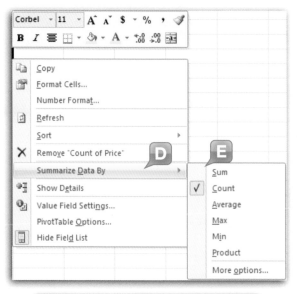 and click the data summary option that best meets your needs.

CONTINUE

- **Sum:** Sums the values of all cells in the range **F**.

	A	B	C
1		Values	
2	Row Labels ▾	Sum of Coupon	Sum of Price
3	Cash	1	521.53
4	Check	2	401.47
5	Credit	2	1902.57
6	Debit	1	118.16
7	Grand Total	6	2943.73

- **Count:** Displays the total number of cells in the selected range that contain a value **G**.

	A	B	C
1		Values	
2	Row Labels ▾	Sum of Coupon	Count of Price
3	Cash	1	3
4	Check	2	2
5	Credit	2	3
6	Debit	1	2
7	Grand Total	6	10

- **Average:** Calculates the average of the values of the cells in the selected range **H**.

	A	B	C
1		Values	
2	Row Labels ▾	Sum of Coupon	Average of Price
3	Cash	1	173.8433333
4	Check	2	200.735
5	Credit	2	634.19
6	Debit	1	59.08
7	Grand Total	6	294.373

- **Max:** Displays the highest value in the selected range of cells **I**.

	A	B	C
1		Values	
2	Row Labels ▾	Sum of Coupon	Max of Price
3	Cash	1	224.93
4	Check	2	331.62
5	Credit	2	1832.28
6	Debit	1	96.08
7	Grand Total	6	1832.28

- **Min:** Displays the lowest value in the selected range of cells 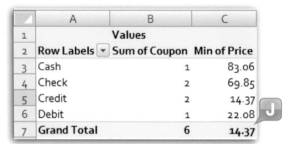.

	A	B	C
1		Values	
2	Row Labels ▾	Sum of Coupon	Min of Price
3	Cash	1	83.06
4	Check	2	69.85
5	Credit	2	14.37
6	Debit	1	22.08
7	Grand Total	6	14.37

- **Product:** Displays the product obtained when each value in the range is multiplied by the next .

	A	B	C
1		Values	
2	Row Labels ▾	Sum of Coupon	Product of Price
3	Cash	1	3989500.726
4	Check	2	23163.657
5	Credit	2	1472365.973
6	Debit	1	2121.4464
7	Grand Total	6	2.88651E+20

- **More Options:** Launches the **Value Field Settings** dialog box 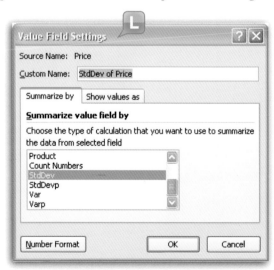, which provides access to additional options and settings.

Value Field Settings [?][X]

Source Name: Price

Custom Name: StdDev of Price

Summarize by | Show values as

Summarize value field by

Choose the type of calculation that you want to use to summarize the data from selected field

Product
Count Numbers
StdDev
StdDevp
Var
Varp

Number Format | OK | Cancel

STOP

Change How Data is Displayed in a PivotTable   89

31 | Group Data Within a PivotTable

Difficulty:

There may be times when the sheer quantity of data you are reviewing or analyzing in a PivotTable makes it difficult to isolate the information you need. In these cases, it may be helpful to group the data.

Grouping data doesn't eliminate the more detailed information, it merely collapses it into units that can be reviewed or expanded to show the original components. For example, if you are looking at twenty years of data broken down by day, month, and year, you might want to group the information by month, quarter, year, or even decade. Once grouped, each group receives its own dropdown menu that allows you to expand or collapse the detail.

SEE ALSO: CREATE A PIVOTTABLE

Sum of Amount	Column Labels			
Row Labels	1123	2354	3543	Grand Total
3-Jan	111	81		192
1-Feb		135		135
2-Feb		120		120
3-Feb			1083.75	1083.75
1-Feb	60			60
1-Mar		55		55
2-Mar		57	44	101
3-Mar			317.25	317.25
1-Apr	15			15
2-Apr	3			3
3-Apr	2.75			2.75
4-Apr	22	27		49
5-Apr		28		28
1-May		57	89.25	146.25
2-May			272	272
Grand Total	213.75	560	1806.25	2580

Sum of Amount	Column Labels			
Row Labels	1123	2354	3543	Grand Total
⊞ Jan	111	81		192
⊟ Feb				
1-Feb	60	135		195
2-Feb		120		120
3-Feb			1083.75	1083.75
⊞ Mar		112	361.25	473.25
⊞ Apr	42.75	55		97.75
⊞ May		57	361.25	418.25
Grand Total	213.75	560	1806.25	2580

Sum of Amount	Column Labels			
Row Labels	1123	2354	3543	Grand Total
⊟ Qtr1				
Jan	111	81		192
Feb	60	255	1083.75	1398.75
Mar		112	361.25	473.25
⊞ Qtr2	42.75	112	361.25	516
Grand Total	213.75	560	1806.25	2580

Step-by-Step

Group Data in a PivotTable

1. Right-click any cell in the row or column that contains the data you want to group .

2. Click the **Group** option **B** in the context menu.

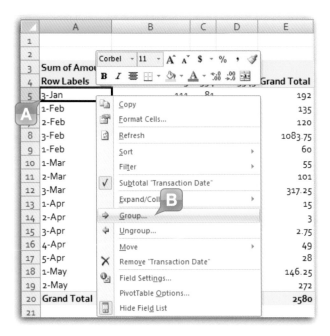

3. In the **Grouping** dialog box :

- Adjust the values in **Auto** textboxes D (in the illustration below the parameters are dates because the data being grouped is dates) OR uncheck the **Auto** checkboxes E to ignore these fields.

- Select an option from the **By** selection box F to group your data by that increment.

4. Review your data, now grouped in the way you identified **G**.

3	Sum of Amount	Column Labels ▾			
4	Row Labels ▾	1123	2354	3543	Grand Total
5	Jan		111	81	192
6	Feb		60	255	1083.75	1398.75
7	Mar			112	361.25	473.25
8	Apr	42.75	55		97.75
9	May			57	361.25	418.25
10	Grand Total	213.75	560	1806.25	2580

32 | Find a Value From Another Table

Difficulty:

Sometimes you are working in one worksheet or table and require a value stored in another table. VLOOKUP is a powerful tool that allows you to do just that. With VLOOKUP, you identify a collection of data to search, look through one column for a value, and return the value in a different column for that row.

For example, an organization receives money from donors to support its various charitable projects. You need to find out how much money a given donor gave you last year. Because there are thousands of donors in your system, and because each donor record contains dozens of pieces of information (name, address, phone number, preferred projects, donation history, etc.), scrolling through pages of information to find the data could take hours. A VLOOKUP for donor Mark Smith returning the YTD_Donations column data would make the process much faster.

> **What Microsoft Calls It:** VLOOKUP

 Step-by-Step

Conduct a VLOOKUP Query

In this example, a Donor Lookup field is created where a donor's name can be entered and the cell containing the VLOOKUP formula returns last year's total donations for that member.

1. Open a worksheet where you want to create a **VLOOKUP** field.

2. In this example, a label field is created 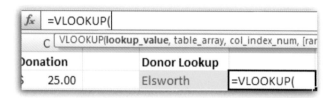, and the field where the name can be entered is highlighted green for clarity. The field where the donor's name can be entered is E2, and the **VLOOKUP** resides in F2.

	A	B	C	D	E
					Donor Lookup
1	Level	Donor	Donation		Donor Lookup
2	Member	Gayle	$ 25.00		Elsworth
3	Member	Morton	$ 954.00		
4	Honor	Elsworth	$ 8,846.00		
5	Bronze	Grandy	$13,485.00		

E3

fx =VLOOKUP(

VLOOKUP(lookup_value, table_array, col_index_num, [ran

Donation	Donor Lookup	
25.00	Elsworth	=VLOOKUP(

3. Enter a sample value in the field that is referenced by the **VLOOKUP** function. It should be a value near the top of the data list that quickly shows whether or not the formula is entered correctly when you complete it. In this case, Elsworth was entered.

4. Select the cell where the VLOOKUP formula will reside. In this example, that is cell F2.

CONTINUE

5. Type **=VLOOKUP(** in the formula bar .

6. The **lookup_value** is the cell where the term searched for is entered. In this example, cell E2 is where the donor's name is entered.

7. The **table_array** should be the area of data that is searched for the lookup value and the returned value (in this case the donation amount). In this example, that is cells B2 (the top value-containing cell in the Donor column) through C21 (the bottom value-containg cell in the Donation column).

8. The **col_index_num** is the number of the column in the selected array searched for the returned value. Column C is the one searched, and while it is Column 3 in your table (counting from left to right), it is only column 2 of the array you identified for the VLOOKUP. **2** (for Column 2) is entered here.

9. The **range_lookup value** is either TRUE or FALSE. Entering a value of TRUE requires the searched column (the donor column in this example) to be in ascending order, and causes Excel to search for an approximate match. A selection of FALSE eliminates the ascending order requirement but searches only for an exact match. In this example, FALSE is selected.

10. Close the parentheses in the formula.

11. Press the **ENTER** key on your keyboard.

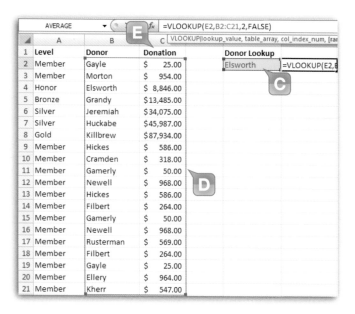

12. Review the result .

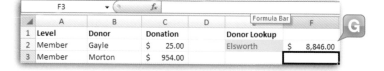

⚠️ If you plan to apply your VLOOKUP formula to multiple cells, make sure your table array arguments are absolute references.

33 | Find the Tab that Allows Access to Macros and VBA

Difficulty:

If you frequently use workbooks and worksheets that include macros, or if you are an advanced user accustomed to utilizing advanced macro and VBA functions, the default settings in Excel 2007 may be somewhat limiting. All VBA content is disabled by default in this version of the program. This includes all macros, as macros are coded in VBA.

For example, when you open a workbook that contains macros you might see a Security Alert message. Alternately, you may be unable to find the **Macro Dialog Box**. Enabling the **Developer** tab addresses these problems.

> **What Microsoft Calls It:** Enabling the Developer Tab, Enabling VBA, Enabling Visual Basic for Applications

 Step-by-Step

Enable the Developer Tab

Use this solution to record macros or if you routinely access and edit workbooks that contain macros.

1. Click the **Office** button.

2. Click the **Excel Options** button.

3. Make sure the **Popular** options are active and visible.

4. Click the **Show Developer tab in the Ribbon** checkbox **A** so it is checked.

5. Click the **OK** button.

 Caution: Be careful when you modify your macro security settings. Macros are very powerful. Enabling the **Developer** tab opens your system to potential security hazards.

Quickest Click: Enable Macros
Use this solution to enable macros in a particular trusted workbook.
   If you receive a **Security Warning** B on your **Message Bar** C when opening a macro-enabled workbook, click the **Options** button D to launch the **Microsoft Security Options** dialog box E. Click the **Enable this content** radio button F and then click the **OK** button G to enable macros in this workbook only.

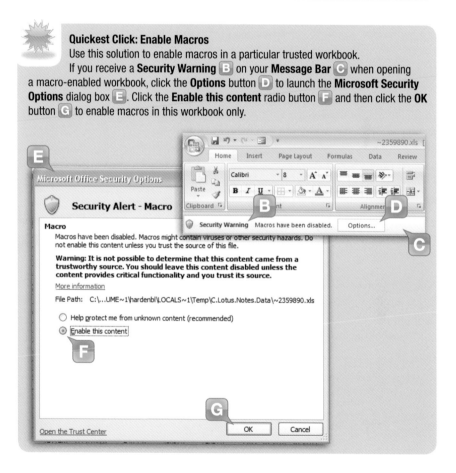

34 | Record a Macro

Difficulty:

Many Excel users perform the same tasks or operations on an hourly, daily, weekly, or monthly basis. Repeating the same sets of actions to set up a worksheet or get data in a position to be analyzed is monotonous and invites errors. Macros automate repetitive tasks to speed up and streamline working in Excel.

Macros are collections of commands that perform pre-determined actions in your worksheet. Macros can either be recorded (Excel tracks and documents your actions) or programmed (written in VB—Visual Basic—code in a special editor).

Macros can be used for a number of different functions. For example, you can record a series of actions that sets up your spreadsheet to look a certain way or organizes your data in a particular fashion. For example, if you always make the same changes to a spreadsheet you review every week, you can record the actions for setting up the worksheet once, save it as a macro, and then make those changes with a single click going forward.

Macros can also be used to run a series of calculations on a collection of data. For example, if you always prepare a report by multiplying the items in Column A by the corresponding items in Column B, you can set up a macro that performs that action each time you need it done with one keystroke.

See Also: Find the Tab that Allows Access to Macros and VBA

Step-by-Step

Record a Macro

This macro takes raw sales data from a report and converts it into user-friendly information. The report used in this example has three columns.

- Column A contains the number of the store that made each sale.

- Column B contains the date each sale was made, but the date is expressed in the native Microsoft Excel numeric format, meaning that it is just a series of seemingly random numbers.

- Column C contains the amount of each sale, but the prices are formatted as numbers rather than currency.

	A	B	C
1	Store Number	Transaction Date	Amount
2	1123	39845	15
3	1123	39085	3
4	1123	39085	2.75
5	1123	39085	22
6	2354	39085	27

The goal in this example is to create a macro that converts the Transaction Date data to a standard date format, and the Amount to dollars.

1. Make sure the **Developer** tab is enabled. The tab is enabled if it is visible on the ribbon.

2. Click the **Record Macro** button **A** in the **Code** group on the **Developer** tab.

CONTINUE

3. In the **Record Macro** dialog box:

   - Provide a name for your macro in the **Macro name** field. Create a descriptive name rather than something like "macro1."

   - Identify a shortcut key (it must be a letter) for your macro in the **Shortcut key** textbox. This is the key you press on your keyboard to run your macro after recording it.

   - Choose a location where you want your macro to be stored from the **Store macro in** dropdown .

   - Provide a clear description of what your macro does in the **Description** field so you (and others) can remember its purpose.

4. Click the **OK** button. If there are no problems with your macro information, recording begins immediately. If there are problems (such as if the shortcut key you selected was already in use), correct the problems and then press the **OK** button again.

5. Perform the actions you want to record in your macro. The actions recorded for the sample macro are listed here:

  - Select **Column B**, then use the tools in the **Format Cells** dialog box (accessed from the **Number** group on the **Home** tab), choose to format the data as MM/DD/YYYY.

  - Select **Column C**, then, use the tools in the **Format Cells** dialog box, choose to format the data as currency ($0.00).

6. Click the **Stop Recording** button in the **Code** group on the **Developer** tab.

7. Use the macro any time you have a similar set of data.

Bright idea: Add a macro to your **Quick Access** toolbar. See the **Customize Quick Access Toolbar** tip for complete customization instructions. To access your list of macros during customization, select **Macros** from the **Choose commands from** dropdown menu.

Bookmark Cells and Groups of Cells for Easy Reference

Difficulty:

Some people work with either very large or very complex spreadsheets. Those working with large sheets may find that they frequently reference a particular set of cells that are hundreds or even thousands of rows down (or columns over) in a sheet. People who have particularly complex sheets may have many formulas that often refer to key cells and data. In either case, the users of those sheets might benefit from Named Cells and Ranges.

A named cell is a cell that, while still locatable by its coordinates, also carries a name that the user defines. For example, if you have standard gasoline reimbursements for on-the-road salespeople, you might have a standard per-mile gasoline charge that then has a state-based or regional multiplier attached to it (to account for higher gas prices in some areas than others). Naming a range "Gas-Northeast" would make it very easy to apply that particular range to the relevant salespeople.

A named range is a group of cells that you name. For example, if you have a sheet that covers twenty years worth of data, you may have series of analysis tables that isolate particular months and years. Somewhere hundreds of rows down or columns across is your collection of data covering the month of January for the years 1984–2004. Naming that range "January-84-04" makes locating it much easier than scrolling to find it.

> **What Microsoft Calls It:** Named Cells & Ranges

Step-by-Step

Create a Named Range of Cells

1. Select the cells you want to name .

	BK	BL	BM	BN	BO
	3Q 2002	3Q 2002	3Q 2002	3Q 2002	3Q Avg
394	Target	Finals	Returns	Actuals	1992-2002
395	$10,000.00	$ 9,763.00	($1,212.00)	$ 8,551.00	9893
396	$13,000.00	$14,558.00	($2,678.00)	$11,880.00	12506
397	$ 5,000.00	$ 8,954.00	($3,002.00)	$ 5,952.00	4429
398	$ 1,500.00	$22,669.00	($8,764.00)	$13,905.00	1235
399	$25,000.00	$37,884.00	($300.00)	$37,584.00	225523

2. Click the **Formulas** tab.

3. In the **Defined Names** group, click the **Define Name** button .

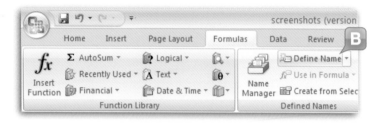

4. Type a name for your range in the **Name** textbox . Note that names must begin with an underscore or letter and cannot contain spaces.

5. Select the scope of the range from the **Scope** dropdown menu . The scope defines where the name will be saved. You can have it apply to a whole workbook (so that range name typed in any sheet in the workbook will bring you to that location) or you can confine it to a single sheet.

6. Click the **OK** button .

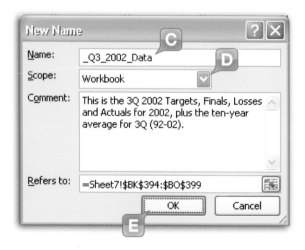

36 | Insert a Chart

Difficulty:

Charts provide an easy-to-assemble but clear and persuasive illustration of your data. Excel offers a variety of charts in both two-dimensional and three-dimensional formats.

For example, if you want to illustrate which sales associates have contributed the most sales during a set period, a chart would convey that information better than raw data.

SEE ALSO: APPENDIX B

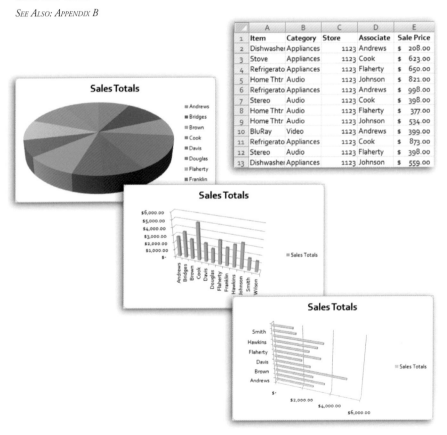

Step-by-Step

Insert a Chart

Use this method when you want more chart options or if you want to fine-tune the way the data appears.

1. Select the data you want to chart **A**. Make sure you highlight header rows and columns if you want the labels included on the chart.

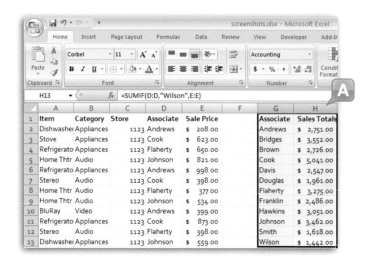

CONTINUE

2. In the **Charts** group on the **Insert** tab, click the dropdown button for the chart type you want to use. To access charts not shown in the box, click the **Other Charts** button **B**, or click the **Charts** dialog box launcher **C**. **Column D** was selected for this example.

3. Select the specific chart from the dropdown menu panel that appears. **3D Pyramid E** was selected for this example.

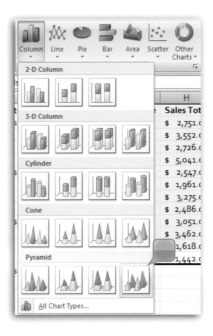

4. Review the chart, and make any changes you need to the design or layout.

Quickest Click: Insert a Chart
Use this method when you want a quick visual snapshot of your data. Highlight the data you want to chart, then press the **F11** key on your keyboard. Excel chooses what it thinks is the best chart type for your data, and a basic chart is created on a new worksheet added to the left of the sheet that contained the data you charted.

37 | Determine if Your Data Shows a Relevant Trend

Difficulty:

Charts reveal a great deal about your data in a dynamic and accessible format. Sometimes, though, there are swings in the data that make it difficult to discern if there is an important trend in the information. Trendlines perform calculations behind the scenes and provide an indicator of the direction your data is moving to help make the big picture clear.

Including a trendline in your charts may help illustrate both the size and direction of changes in your data. They are also useful in forecasting future or past values based on available data.

For example, you may have a workbook that contains a full twelve months of a factory's widget production. Even after graphing the data, it is just not clear if production went up or down over the course of the year. By inserting a trendline, you can see if your sales went up, and, if so, by how much.

	A	B
1	Month	Total Production
2	January	6613954
3	February	7456838
4	March	7517093
5	April	6689126
6	May	5956554
7	June	5822540
8	July	6460424
9	August	7292989
10	September	6967066
11	...ber	6622203
	...mber	5187193
	...mber	4959537

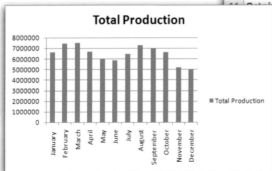

What Microsoft Calls It: Add a Trendline to Your Chart

Step-by-Step

Add a Trendline to Your Chart

1. Right-click on any data bar in the chart and select **Add Trendline** from the menu that appears 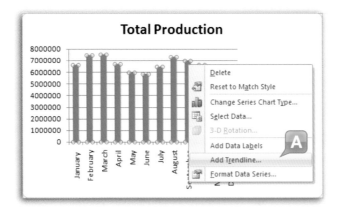.

2. For a basic trendline indicating the general direction of your data, click the radio button to the left of **Linear** 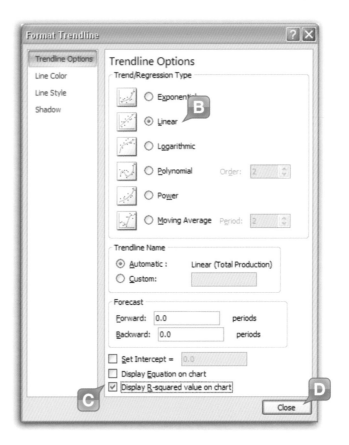 **B** to select that option.

3. Click the **Display R-squared value on chart** checkbox **C**.

4. Click the **Close** button **D**.

5. Review your chart with the trendline in place **E**. Note that the R-squared value on the trendline is 0.3429. In the simplest terms, this means that the downward trend the line indicates is roughly 34% accurate—meaning that while there is an apparent drop in production, it is not statistically significant. The closer a trend is to "1," or 100%, the more accurate it is. Most trends should not be considered significant until they are at least 0.5, or 50%.

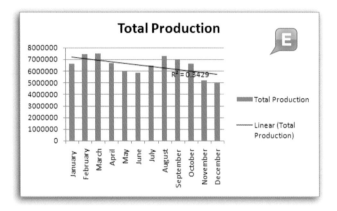

 Bright Idea: Because Excel 2007 offers a live preview option with this feature, drag the **Format Trendline** dialog box off to the side and click through the various trendline options to see how they change the trendline's shape as it changes how your data is analyzed.

38 | Create a Chart From Your PivotTable

Difficulty:

PivotTables do a great job of helping you identify trends and patterns in your data. Sometimes you may need a more visual representation of the information—whether for a PowerPoint slide, a meeting agenda, a report, or faster analysis.

For example, you might have thousands of donors listed with their annual gifts. A PivotTable may not help you see which donors gave the most, or how many donors gave you donations at various giving tiers. A PivotChart gives you the snapshot of that data that you need.

	A	B	C	D
1	Level	Donor	Donation	Donation Date
2	Member	Gayle	$ 25.00	1/1/2008
3	Member	Morton	$ 954.00	1/1/2008
4	Honor	Elsworth	$ 8,846.00	1/1/2008
5	Bronze	Grandy	$13,485.00	1/1/2008
6	Silver	Jeremiah	$34,075.00	1/1/2008
7	Silver	Huckabe	$45,987	
8	Gold	Killbrew	$87,934	
9	Member	Hickes	$ 586	
10	Member	Cramden	$ 318	

	A	B	C
1			
2			
3		Values	
4	Row Labels ▼	Sum of Donation	Count of Donation2
5	Bronze	2241989	133
6	Gold	8090581	111
7	Honor	778114	96
8	Member	1382377	1343
9	Silver	3970193	105
			1788

Sum of Donation

- Bronze
- Gold
- Honor
- Member
- Silver

What Microsoft Calls It: Insert a PivotChart

Step-by-Step

Create a PivotChart

Option:
a. Go directly from your data to a PivotChart (which creates a PivotTable in the process) by clicking a cell within the data you want to chart.
b. Create a PivotChart from an existing PivotTable by clicking any field in the PivotTable to select it.

1. If you selected option **a.** from above, click the lower half of the **PivotTable** combo button **A** in the **Tables** group of the **Insert** tab and select **PivotChart** **B**.

    If you selected option **b.** from above, click the **PivotChart** button **C** in the **Tools** group of the **Options** tab in the highlighted **PivotTable Tools** section of the ribbon.

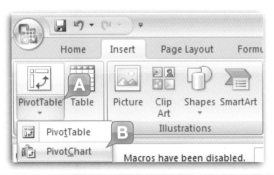

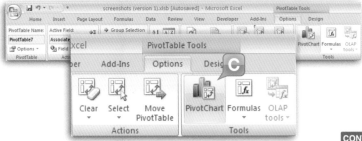

CONTINUE

2. If you chose option **a.**, Excel chooses the chart type it believes is most appropriate to your data.

If you select option **b.**, the **Insert Chart** dialog box **D** appears where you can select the type and subtype of chart you want to insert.

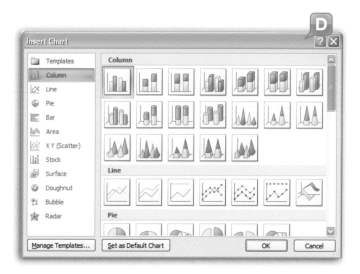

3. Review your chart .

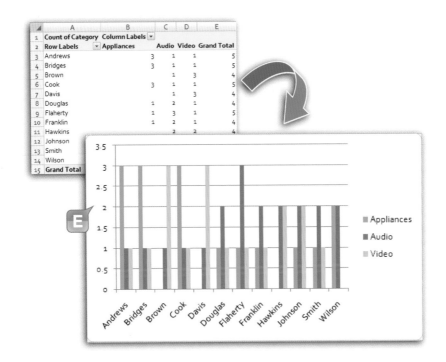

	A	B	C	D	E
1	Count of Category	Column Labels			
2	Row Labels	Appliances	Audio	Video	Grand Total
3	Andrews	3	1	1	5
4	Bridges	3	1	1	5
5	Brown		1	3	4
6	Cook	3	1	1	5
7	Davis		1	3	4
8	Douglas	1	2	1	4
9	Flaherty	1	3	1	5
10	Franklin	1	2	1	4
11	Hawkins		2	2	4
12	Johnson				
13	Smith				
14	Wilson				
15	Grand Total				

Bright Idea: You can change the info displayed just like in a PivotTable. Drag and drop fields to change X axis, Y axis, filter, or the data displayed.

STOP

Create a Chart From Your PivotTable   117

39 Insert a SmartArt Graphic

Difficulty:

Data can be compelling information, but often you need to express it graphically to help others understand what the numbers mean. Photos and ClipArt can create humor or emotional appeal, and charts and graphs are great for demonstrating trends and totals. But what if you need to demonstrate a process or a relationship?

Processes are sometimes complicated and require elements that show relationships. For example, you may need to explain that changes to one element of a project will impact development time, cost, and customer response, and, therefore, revenue. The SmartArt feature helps. The charts and process maps created with this powerful tool provide visually appealing and dynamic images to convey information clearly.

SmartArt graphics are divided into seven categories. Some graphics can be used to express multiple concepts and so appear in more than one category. Here is a list of the categories and an explanation for each:

- **All**: This is not a category. By choosing this option you can view all graphics from all categories.
- **List**: These graphics are best used to express static lists of information.
- **Process**: These graphics are best used to express processes and procedures where there are multiple steps with various effects, consequences, and paths.
- **Cycle**: These graphics are best used to express cyclical events or repetitive processes.
- **Hierarchy**: These graphics are best used to display groups or lists where one item takes precedence over another.
- **Relationship**: These graphics are best used to display information that is connected to or dependent on other information, resources, or processes.
- **Matrix**: These graphics are best used to show the relationship of information or components to a whole.
- **Pyramid**: These graphics combine hierarchy and relationship. Higher levels depend on the items in the levels below.

Step-by-Step

Insert a SmartArt Graphic

1. Click the **SmartArt** button **A** in the **Illustrations** group of the **Insert** tab.

2. In the **Choose a SmartArt Graphic** dialog box, select a **SmartArt** category from the left panel **B** to reveal the graphic options for that category in the center panel **C**.

3. Click a graphic **D** to reveal a sample of what it will look like once it is inserted in the right panel **E**. This panel also includes a brief description of the graphic and the information it would best be used to convey.

4. When you have found the graphic you want to insert, make sure it is selected and then click the **OK** button **F**.

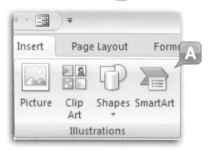

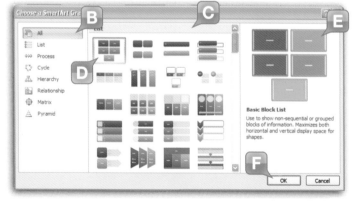

40

Configure a SmartArt Graphic

Difficulty:

When you are working with SmartArt graphics, it is important to configure them so that they speak to your audience and project the message you intend. For example, do you want to use your company's colors, client or vendor colors, or colors that best convey your message? Should your look and feel be smooth and rounded or crisp and shadowed?

All of these choices are ones you will have to make on your own, but once you have made them, the tools Microsoft provides in the SmartArt design panel will make implementing them easy.

When you insert or select a SmartArt graphic, two new tabs appear: the SmartArt Tools Design tab and the Smart Art Tools Format tab. The Design tab options let you make color and layout selections for the graphic as a whole, while the Format tab lets you drill down and make choices about the individual shape and WordArt elements in the graphic.

Step-by-Step

Configure a SmartArt Graphic

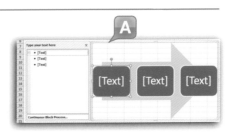

1. Select the graphic so it is active. You can tell a graphic is selected or active if you can see the border around the items **A**.

2. Select an area marked **[Text]** **B**, and begin typing to enter your information into the graphic **C**.

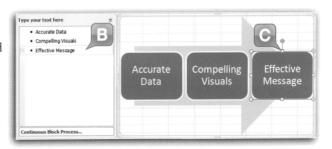

3. Once you have entered all of your text elements, use the tools on the **SmartArt Tools Design** and **SmartArt Tools Format** tabs to adjust the appearance of your graphic.

Design Tab:

- **Create Graphic Group**: Here you can insert additional items (the **Add Bullet** button), elements (the **Add Shape** button), or adjust the direction of the graphic.

- **Layouts Group**: In this section you can adjust the entire graphic.

- **SmartArt Styles Group**: These tools let you change the look and feel of your graphic (borders, drop shadows, rotation, reflection etc.).

- **Reset**: This button returns the graphic to its original state before you started making adjustments.

Format Tab:

- **Shapes**: These tools let you select an element or group of elements in your graphic and change their shape. In the example at right, you could change the rounded squares containing text to circles.

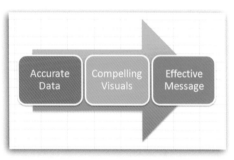

- **Shape Styles**: Here you can adjust the look and feel of an element or group of elements. In the example at right, you could change the rounded squares from a white outline with blue fill to a blue outline with a white fill, and a shadow.

- **WordArt Styles**: Most SmartArt graphic text is displayed in WordArt. As a result, you can change the appearance of the text with many settings, including color, outline, shadow, 3D, and more.

- **Arrange**: This button gives you access to change the arrangement of the elements within your SmartArt graphic, and the arrangement of multiple graphics on the page (if you have more than one).

- **Size**: This button gives you access to tools that will allow you to change the physical (print) size of the SmartArt graphic.

STOP

41

Select and Apply a Theme to Your Documents

Difficulty: ●●○○

When you create a collection of documents—such as a PowerPoint presentation, an Excel spreadsheet with charts, and a Word meeting agenda—you will want them all to share the same look and feel. When your documents have a unified and polished appearance, they make a more professional, positive impression. This is easy to accomplish with Themes.

Document Themes are sets of colors, fonts, and other formatting details that together give your document collection a cohesive identity.

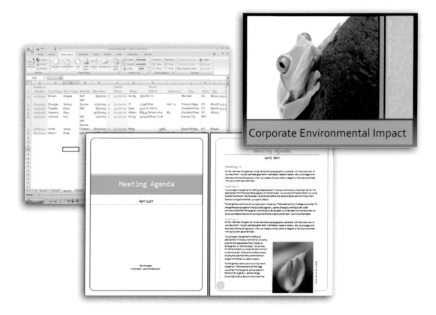

Corporate Environmental Impact

 What Microsoft Calls It: Document Themes or Themes.

Step-by-Step

Select and Apply a Document Theme

1. Click the **Themes** button in the **Themes** panel of the **Page Layout** tab.

2. Hover over themes in the **Built In** selection panel **B** to preview the theme on your worksheet. NOTE: UNLESS YOU HAVE A VISIBLE CHART/GRAPH OR SMARTART ITEM, SOME CHANGES TO CELLS WITH BACKGROUND FILLS, COLORED TEXT, OR STYLE SETS MAY BE CONFINED TO FONT SELECTION AND THEREFORE WILL BE HARD TO SEE.

Option: If you have an active internet connection you may choose to click the **More Themes on Microsoft Office Online** link **C** to view and download additional themes.

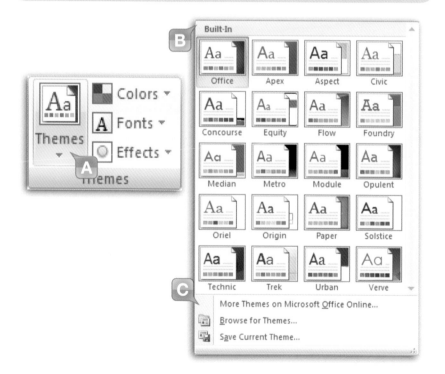

4. When you have found the theme that suits your needs, just click to apply.

5. Examine your results **D E F**, and, if applicable, review your associated documents (such as an agenda in Word or your presentation in PowerPoint) to be sure you like the look there as well.

6. Save your worksheet with the changes.

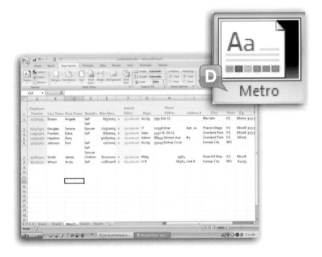

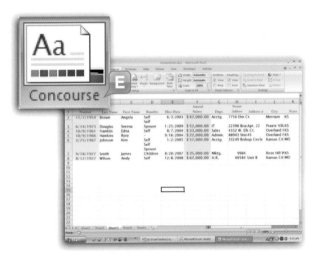

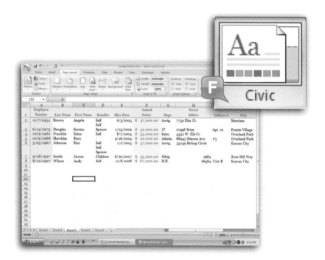

42

Make Your Own Theme

Difficulty:  ●●○○

There will be times when the built-in document themes are not sufficient to meet your design needs. You may need to create specific color combinations to match your corporate colors or logo, or those of your clients. A particular marketing effort might require a specific look and feel or particular design elements.

 What Microsoft Calls It: Customize Document Themes

Step-by-Step

Customizing a Theme

1. Apply the theme that best matches your needs to your document.

2. Make your adjustments to color, font, and design elements using the tools available on the Ribbon:
   - On the **Home** tab in the **Styles** and **Cells** group.
   - On the **Insert** tab in the **Text** group.
   - On the **Page Layout** tab in the **Themes** group.

3. Click the **Themes** button 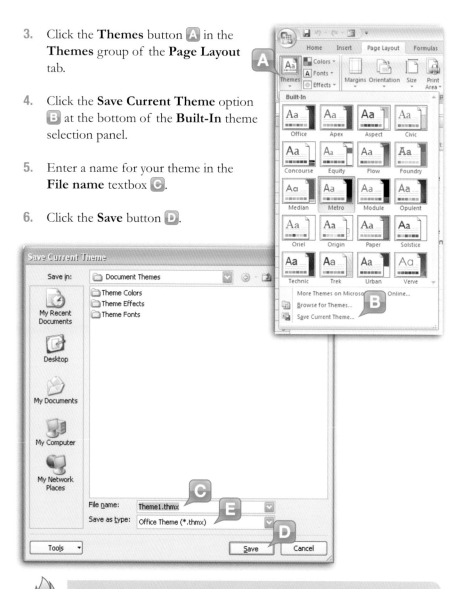 in the **Themes** group of the **Page Layout** tab.

4. Click the **Save Current Theme** option at the bottom of the **Built-In** theme selection panel.

5. Enter a name for your theme in the **File name** textbox.

6. Click the **Save** button.

Hot Tip: You'll notice when you save your theme that the file type (in the **Save as Type** textbox) is **Office Theme(*.thmx)**. This means that your new theme will be available in other Office applications. You may need to make additions or small changes when you use a theme created in another application, but your custom theme will be ready to use for most projects.

STOP

43

Add Information to the Tops or Bottoms of Printed Pages

Difficulty: ⬤◯◯◯

Many of the reports you create are produced on a regular basis. Often it is valuable to know which version of a report you are looking at, as most business decisions need to be based on the most current data.

Headers and footers provide an excellent means of tracking versioning data, including revision dates and author changes. They also can make deciphering report information easier through the inclusion of navigation aids like page numbers, footnotes, and legends.

 Insert a Header and Footer

 Step-by-Step

Insert and Configure Headers and Footers

1. Click the **Header & Footer** button **A** in the **Text** group of the **Insert** tab. This converts your workbook to page layout view and launches the **Header & Footer Tools Design** tab **B**.

2. Set up your header and footer using the tools in the **Design** tab groups.

- **Header & Footer** group **C**: Click one of these buttons to select pre-set header and footer formatting options.
- **Header & Footer Elements** group **D**: Insert and configure only the elements you want, one at a time.
  - ○ **Page Number**: Displays the page number.
  - ○ **Number of Pages**: Displays the total number of pages in the sheet.
  - ○ **Current Date**: Displays the current date each time the sheet is opened.
  - ○ **Current Time**: Displays the current time when the sheet is opened.
  - ○ **File Path**: Displays the full path to the file's location, including network locations.
  - ○ **File Name**: Displays the full file name.
  - ○ **Sheet Name**: Displays the name of the individual sheet.
  - ○ **Picture**: Inserts a picture.
  - ○ **Format Picture**: Becomes active if you have a picture inserted and selected and allows you configure the image.

- **Navigation** group **E**: Move between the header and footer.
- **Options** group **F**: Select how and on which pages headers and footers appear and how they will print.

 Caution: Each worksheet has its own header, so make sure the worksheet to which you want to apply a header is active.

44 | Page Setup

Difficulty: ●○○○

Excel's work area is designed to make data entry and analysis efficient and user-friendly. This focus toward on-screen navigation becomes apparent as soon as you try to print your sheet.

Configuring your print page can be tricky and confusing, but Microsoft has provided some tools to make this configuration relatively easy—once you know what they are and how to use them.

There are two ways to approach Page Setup: Using the **Print Preview** window and using the **Page Setup** dialog box.

While making adjustments on the Print Preview screen is the fastest method for preparing your sheet to print; the arguably better way is to adjust those settings before you get there. By setting up your sheet to consistently print in a particular way with particular settings, you save yourself time and effort, and you save time and effort for your colleagues who may also need to print that sheet. 💡

SEE ALSO: PRINT MULTIPLE WORKSHEETS

Step-by-Step

Page Setup Using the Page Setup Dialog Box Options

1. Launch the **Page Setup** dialog box using either the **Page Setup** dialog box launcher **A** in the **Page Setup** group of the **Page Layout** tab or the **Page Setup** button **B** on the Print Preview screen.

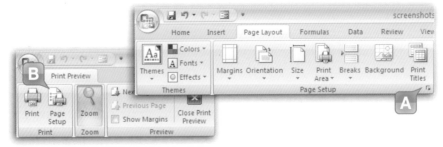

2. Make your formatting selections on the Page, Margins, Header/Footer and Sheet tabs.

    - **Page** 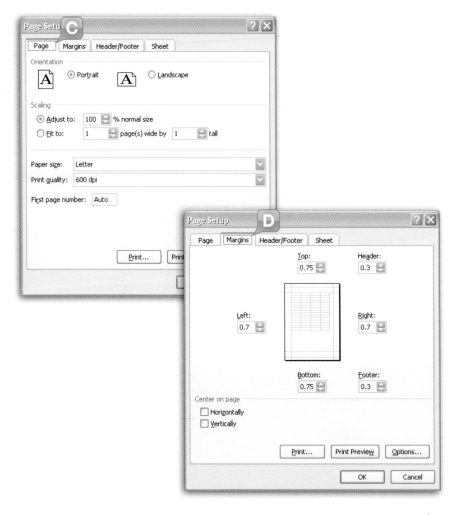**C**: The options on this tab allow you to set basic page layout and printing preferences.

    - **Margins D**: Here you can set page margins and header and footer size measurements.

CONTINUE

- **Header/Footer** E: On this tab you can create a header and/or footer. You can also determine the Header and Footer dimensions and the pages on which they occur.

- **Sheet** F: These selections allow you to define the print area, select rows and/or columns to be repeated on each page, select items to be printed or hidden, and determine page print order for worksheets that take up two or more pages vertically and horizontally.

3. Click the **OK** button.

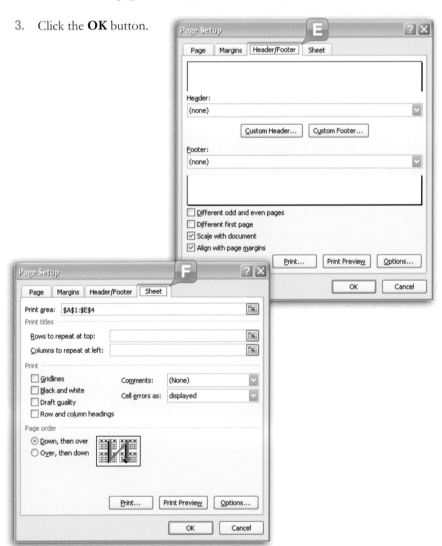

Bright Idea: The **Page Setup** dialog box can be accessed from the **Print Preview** window, so you can combine the two methods for ease of use *and* persistent settings to make future printing fast, easy and correct.

45 | Choose Which Part of Your Worksheet to Print

Difficulty:

There are times when you only need to print a portion of your worksheet rather than the whole thing. In those instances you can designate a specific portion or portions for printing.

Different reports or meetings may require that you print different areas of the same worksheet for several uses. In order to print only what you want or need, clear the print area between each new print job.

What Microsoft Calls It: Setting a print area, Clearing a print area.

Step-by-Step

Using the Page Setup Dialog Box to Set a Print Area

1. Click the **Page Setup** dialog box launcher .

2. Click the **Sheet** tab B.

3. Click the **Print Area** action button C.

4. Click and drag on your worksheet to select the area you want to print D.

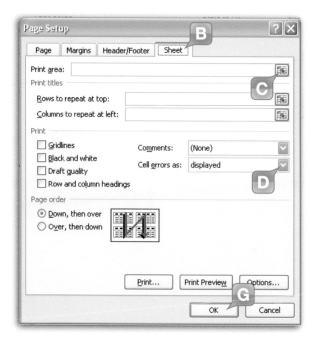

5. The selected area will be displayed as absolute cell references in the **Page Setup Print area:** dialog box 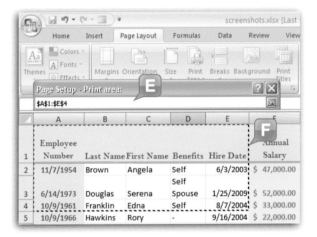, and surrounded by a dotted line **F**.

6. When finished, press the **ENTER** key on your keyboard.

7. Click the **OK** button **G**.

Bright Idea: Select non-adjacent columns and rows for printing by holding the **CTRL** key on your keyboard while you select them. Note that each segment of non-adjacent data prints on its own page.

Quickest Click: Use the Print Area Button to Define a Print Area
First, highlight the cells you want to print . Then, click the **Print Area** button in the **Page Setup** group of the **Page Layout** tab and select **Set Print Area** .

Quickest Click: Clearing a Print Area
Click the **Print Area** button in the **Page Setup** group of the **Page Layout** tab and select **Clear Print Area** .

46 | Print Multiple Worksheets

Difficulty: ⬤◯◯◯

When your workbook contains multiple worksheets (some of which may contain related PivotTables or charts), you may need to print the entire workbook rather than just a single worksheet.

You can either print the worksheets individually (if you need to make special print selections on each one), or you can choose to print your entire workbook at once.

See Also: Choose Which Part of Your Worksheet to Print, Page Setup, Print to a Specific Number of Pages

⌐ Step-by-Step

Printing Multiple Worksheets

1. Press and hold the **CTRL** key on your keyboard while you click the tabs for the worksheets you want to print **A**, **B**, **C**.

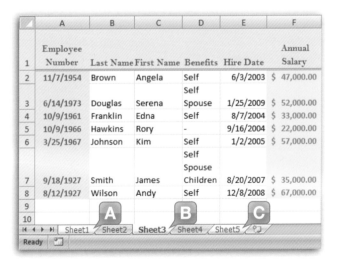

2. Click the **Page Setup** dialog box launcher **D** on the **Page Layout** tab.

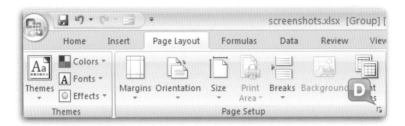

3. Click the **Print Preview** button to confirm that the appropriate pages will print. Note that each worksheet will print on its own page(s).

4. Click the **Print** button.

Bright Idea: In Windows XP, you may also choose to print multiple workbooks at once. To do so, click the **Office** button and choose **Open**. Select multiple documents by holding the **SHIFT** key (for adjacent documents) or **CTRL** key (for non-adjacent documents) on your keyboard while you make your selections, then click the **Tools** button and select **Print**.

STOP

Difficulty: ◉○○○○

Worksheets you prepare may have so many columns (or columns that are so wide) that the sheet stretches across multiple horizontal pages when printed. This can become frustrating and confusing to those trying to review the printed data. Excel has several tools to help with this problem.

The first thing to do is make sure that your page is set up for **Landscape** rather than **Portrait** page **Orientation**. You can quickly adjust this by clicking the **Orientation** button **A** in the **Page Setup** group of the **Page Layout** tab and then clicking the **Landscape** option **B**.

SEE ALSO: CHOOSE WHICH PART OF YOUR WORKSHEET TO PRINT, PAGE SETUP, PRINT MULTIPLE WORKSHEETS

Next, determine where your page breaks are. There are two ways to do this:

- Set your print area. Page breaks are identified with a dashed line **C**.

- Click the **Page Break Preview** button 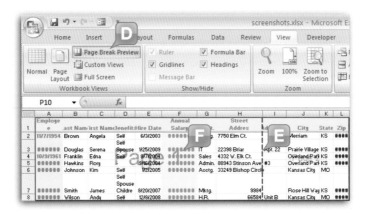 in the **Workbook Views** group of the **View** tab. This reveals the current page breaks (thick blue dashed lines) and the page numbers.

Once you determine that the data does extend beyond a single page, adjust print settings to force the worksheet onto a single page.

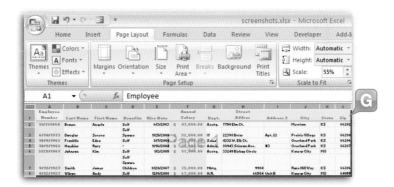

⌐*Step-by-Step*

Print to a Specific Number of Pages

1. Click the **Page Setup** dialog box launcher **H** on the **Page Layout** tab.

2. Click the **Fit to:** radio button **I**.

3. Adjust the pages wide by pages tall numbers in the controls **J**, **K**.

4. Click the **OK** button **L**.

5. Use the **Print Preview** or **Page Break Preview** functions to verify the page breaks appear where you want them to.

Quickest Click: Print to a Specific Number of Pages

While in Page Break Preview, click the **Scale: reduce** button (thus reducing the scale from 100% where you started, which is full-sized) 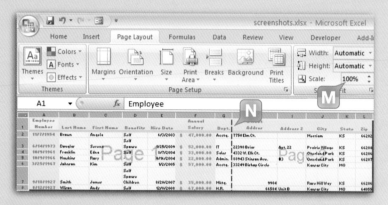 until the page break indicator 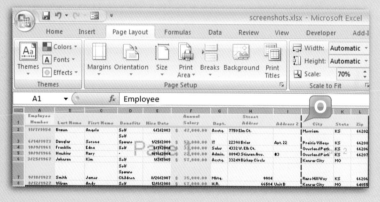 has merged with the page border (the thick blue solid line) and includes all of the data **O**. Use the **Print Preview** function to see how small (and potentially illegible) the adjustment made before you print.

48 | Link Worksheets Together

Difficulty: ●●●○

Worksheets can be linked so that information shared between the two is always identical. This reduces errors and ensures consistency as information only needs to be entered in one place to be available in multiple locations.

For example, donation information might be entered in one sheet by one department, but that donation information might be used by multiple departments. One department tracks gifts for sending out thank you notes, another creates press releases, a third does analysis for case studies and fundraising. Rather than having each of those departments enter the data individually, the necessary information can be linked so that all of the related sheets display it.

> **What Microsoft Calls It:** Linking together workbooks is called **External Reference Links**.

Step-by-Step

Step by Step: Link Worksheets

1. Open both the source  and destination (dependent) **B** workbooks.

Store	Associate	Associate Totals
1123	Andrews	$ 2,751.00
2354	Bridges	$ 3,552.00
3543	Brown	$ 2,726.00
1123	Cook	$ 5,041.00
2354	Davis	$ 2,547.00
3543	Douglas	$ 1,961.00
1123	Flaherty	$ 3,275.00
2354	Franklin	$ 2,486.00
3543	Hawkins	$ 3,051.00
1123	Johnson	$ 3,462.00
2354	Smith	$ 1,618.00
3543	Wilson	$ 1,442.00

2. In the dependent workbook, select a cell 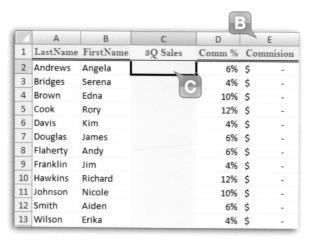 where you want to place the formula that will link that cell to the source data.

	A	B	C	D	E
1	LastName	FirstName	3Q Sales	Comm %	Commision
2	Andrews	Angela		6%	$ -
3	Bridges	Serena		4%	$ -
4	Brown	Edna		10%	$ -
5	Cook	Rory		12%	$ -
6	Davis	Kim		4%	$ -
7	Douglas	James		6%	$ -
8	Flaherty	Andy		6%	$ -
9	Franklin	Jim		4%	$ -
10	Hawkins	Richard		12%	$ -
11	Johnson	Nicole		10%	$ -
12	Smith	Aiden		6%	$ -
13	Wilson	Erika		4%	$ -

3. Enter the formula up to the point where you would refer to the source cell 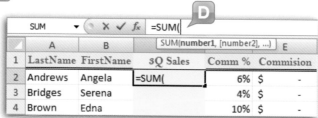.

SUM	▾	✕ ✓ *fx*	=SUM(		
			SUM(number1, [number2], ...)		E
	A	B	3Q Sales	Comm %	Commision
1	LastName	FirstName	=SUM(		
2	Andrews	Angela		6%	$ -
3	Bridges	Serena		4%	$ -
4	Brown	Edna		10%	$ -

CONTINUE ▶

4. Switch to the source workbook and select the cell or data range you need for the formula in the dependent workbook. Excel recognizes you are creating a link and displays the formula in the formula bar **F**.

5. Return to the destination workbook and complete the formula **G**.

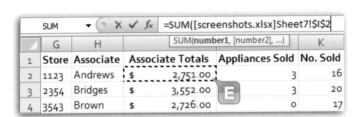

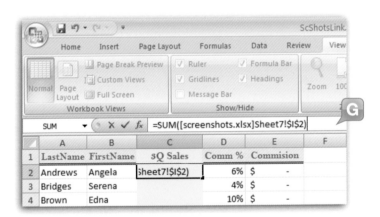

6. Press the **Enter** key on your keyboard to see the cell populated 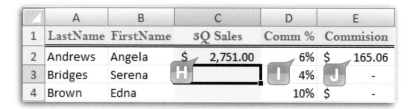 and any related cells compute and populate **I**, **J**.

	A	B	C	D	E
1	LastName	FirstName	3Q Sales	Comm %	Commision
2	Andrews	Angela	$ 2,751.00	6%	$ 165.06
3	Bridges	Serena	H		4%	J -
4	Brown	Edna		10%	$ -

7. Repeat as necessary to complete your links **K**.

	A	B	C	D	E
1	LastName	FirstName	3Q Sales	Comm %	Commision
2	Andrews	Angela	$ 2,751.00	6%	$ 165.06
3	Bridges	Serena	$ 3,552.00	4%	$ 142.08
4	Brown	Edna	$ 2,726.00	10%	$ 272.60
5	Cook	Rory	$ 5,041.00	12%	$ 604.92
6	Davis	Kim	$ 2,547.00	4%	$ 101.88
7	Douglas	James	$ 1,961.00	6%	$ 117.66
8	Flaherty	Andy	$ 3,275.00	6%	$ 196.50
9	Franklin	Jim	$ 2,486.00	4%	$ 99.44
10	Hawkins	Richard	$ 3,051.00	12%	$ 366.12
11	Johnson	Nicole	$ 3,462.00	10%	$ 346.20
12	Smith	Aiden	$ 1,618.00	6%	$ 97.08
13	Wilson	Erika	$ 1,442.00	4%	$ 57.68

Bright Idea: If you plan to apply your links to an entire column of data, change the references from absolute to relative and simply fill down the column.

49

Prepare Your Spreadsheet Data for Use in Access

Difficulty:

While Excel is often used as a database, it is really an analytical tool. Access is a true database program. Because the programs are compatible but not interchangeable, you need to properly prepare your data before you try to move it from one to the other.

Reasons you may need to export information include:

- Your information outgrows Excel in terms of size.

- You want to create and maintain multiple relationships between disparate pieces of information.

- You decide data tracked in Excel should be incorporated into a larger and more comprehensive Access data store. ⚠

Step-by-Step

Prepare Data for Export to Access

1. Adjust your column headers so they contain no spaces or punctuation (underscores can be used to replace spaces, but all other punctuation marks should be removed) **A**.

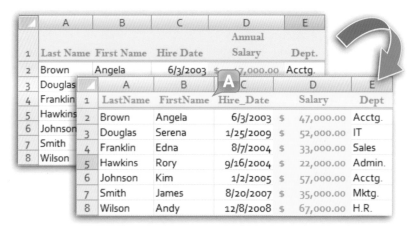

2. If you are exporting your data for import to a database that contains the same or similar information, make sure your column headers match the corresponding ones from the database and that you have the same number of columns as the database for which the information is being prepared.

3. Make sure your worksheet is formatted as a table.

    • Select the data you want to define as a table, including column headers **B**.

    • Click the **Table** button **C** in the **Tables** group of the **Insert** tab to launch the **Create Table** dialog box.

CONTINUE

- Check the **My table has headers** checkbox 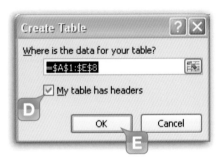.
- Click the **OK** button ■.

4. Eliminate any blank columns, rows, and cells within the data to be exported. You may either eliminate the record containing the empty cells, or you can insert a placeholder value (such as a 0 or NULL). Blank columns and rows at the "ends" of the sheet will be ignored.

Caution: You need to keep the capabilities of each program in mind before you move data between the two, and you need to consider the nature of the data before you move it. For example, Access allows a number of links between various data tables. These links are not necessarily supported or easily demonstrable when you move the information to Excel. You may need to remove duplicate information or split your data into multiple sheets to create the most effective export.

STOP

50 | Pull Data from a Website or Network Location

Difficulty: ●●●○

Sometimes the data you want or need is close at hand—an exported CSV file or even another Excel workbook from which you can import data. Other times, though, the data may be a bit more remote.

Sometimes the data you need may sit on a networked drive and cannot be moved. A consultant may have a large capacity portable hard drive that holds a good deal of information you need but for which you do not have enough room on your local machine. There may even be times when the desired information is on the internet.

For example, you may have an old data system that was retired several years ago but the data from which was exported to a series of large ungainly files kept on a shared drive on your company network. You cannot copy the information to your local machine, but you need to get to it so you can query the historical sales data it includes. Knowing how to connect to external data such as that would save you a good deal of time printing it and re-entering it into a more contemporary system.

 What Microsoft Calls It: Query an External Data Source

Step-by-Step

Query an External Data Source

In this example, GNP data will be retrieved from the World Bank's public website.

1. Open a new worksheet.

2. Click the **From Web** button  in the **Get External Data** group of the **Data** tab.

3. A special **New Web Query** browser window will open. Type the URL of the page from which you want to retrieve data in the address bar **B** and press the ENTER key on your keyboard.

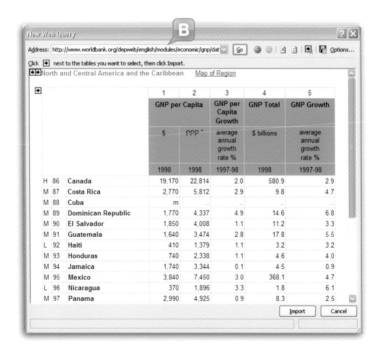

4. Click the yellow-boxed-arrow associated with the data you want to import C. The yellow box will turn green when you hover over it with your mouse, and then convert to a checkmark D after you have clicked it.

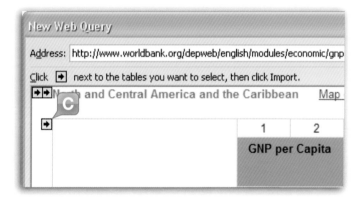

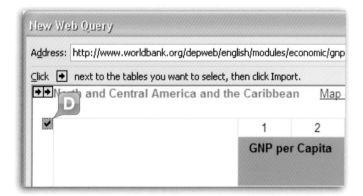

5. Click the **Import** button.

6. In the **Import Data** dialog box, select the **Existing Worksheet** radio button (since you created a new one just for this data back in Step 1).

7. Select the cell where the imported data will start its fill. The data will fill to the right and down as far as it needs to go to import all of it. In this example, the fill was started at cell A1.

8. Click the **OK** button F.

9. Review your imported data G.

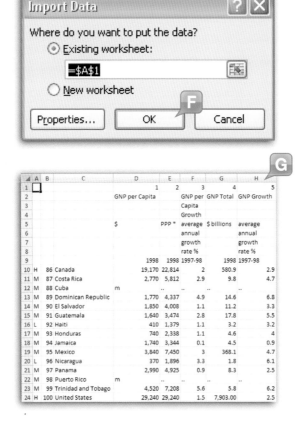

51 | Personalize and Customize Documents

Difficulty:

Mail Merge is a tool in Microsoft Word that allows you to merge a list of data stored in a data source (an Excel spreadsheet, an Access database, a comma-separated-value text file, etc.) with fields in a document.

For example, you may be getting ready to send out a letter inviting people to your yearly donor appreciation banquet. Your spreadsheet could include the address information that would make it easy to generate all of the envelopes quickly and easily. In addition, the worksheet (or another worksheet) might contain the first and last name, honorific (such as "Mr." or "Mrs."), donation amount, or a project the donated funds supported so you could create a very personalized invitation letter.

There are several benefits to using a mail merge to create your documents.

- The process can save you a great deal of time and effort.
- Data can be stored one place and sent to you in a single ready-to-use file.
- Errors are reduced as you are not retyping information already entered.
- Personalized communication tends to yield better results than form letters.

What Microsoft Calls It: Mail Merge

 Step-by-Step

Create a Mail Merge with a Microsoft Word Document

In this example, an Excel spreadsheet is configured to provide content for an invitation to a yearly donor appreciation event.

1. Configure the Excel spreadsheet so that all data to be used in the merge is in columns.

2. Make sure that each column header contains only alphanumeric characters. Words may be separated by an underscore 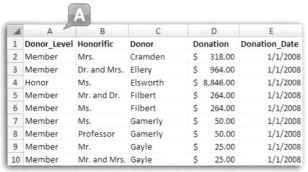, but no other punctuation characters should be used.

	A	B	C	D	E
1	Donor_Level	Honorific	Donor	Donation	Donation_Date
2	Member	Mrs.	Cramden	$ 318.00	1/1/2008
3	Member	Dr. and Mrs.	Ellery	$ 964.00	1/1/2008
4	Honor	Ms.	Elsworth	$ 8,846.00	1/1/2008
5	Member	Mr. and Dr.	Filbert	$ 264.00	1/1/2008
6	Member	Ms.	Filbert	$ 264.00	1/1/2008
7	Member	Ms.	Gamerly	$ 50.00	1/1/2008
8	Member	Professor	Gamerly	$ 50.00	1/1/2008
9	Member	Mr.	Gayle	$ 25.00	1/1/2008
10	Member	Mr. and Mrs.	Gayle	$ 25.00	1/1/2008

3. Save the workbook.

4. In Microsoft Word, prepare the document into which you intend to insert the merge data.

5. Click the **Start Mail Merge** dropdown button **B** in the **Start Mail Merge** group of the **Mailings** tab.

6. Select **Step by Step Mail Merge Wizard** **C**.

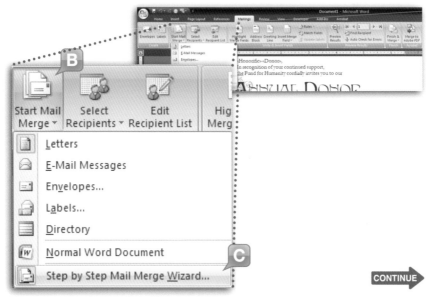

CONTINUE

7. Follow the steps of the Mail Merge wizard.

8. In Step 3 of the wizard, identify the worksheet you just created as your data source.

9. Position your cursor where you would like to insert a merge field.

10. In Step 4, click the **More Items** option 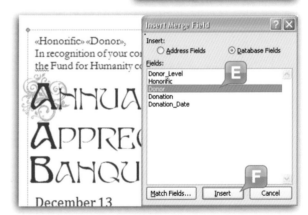 in the **Mail Merge** panel.

11. Select the field you want to insert in the **Fields** window.

12. Click the **Insert** button.

13. Repeat steps 9 through 12 as often as necessary to insert all required merge fields.

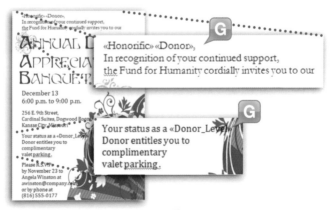

14. Click the **Next: Preview your letters** link .

15. Review the data in the merge fields .

16. Click the **Next: Complete the merge** link .

Bright Idea: Use Mail Merge to populate fields in documents besides letters. The name "mail merge" is somewhat misleading as the functionality is not limited to mail or even to correspondence. The merged data can be addresses for envelopes and labels, contact and personalization information for letters and emails, product information for flyers and catalogs, honoree information for certificates and diplomas—the possibilities are virtually endless.

STOP

Difficulty: ●○○○○

There are times when you want to access a particular command or series of menu options with one easy one-click.

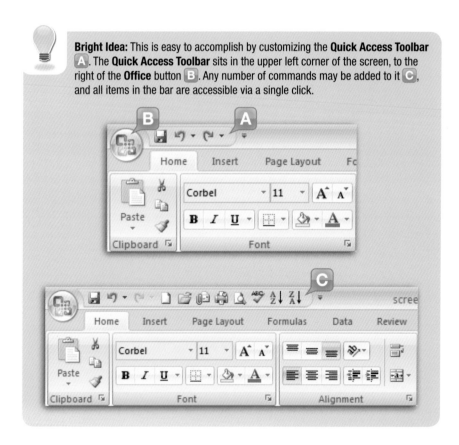

Bright Idea: This is easy to accomplish by customizing the **Quick Access Toolbar** . The **Quick Access Toolbar** sits in the upper left corner of the screen, to the right of the **Office** button **B**. Any number of commands may be added to it **C**, and all items in the bar are accessible via a single click.

Step-by-Step

Customize the Quick Access Toolbar

Use this option if you want a broad selection of items added to your **Quick Access Toolbar**.

1. Click the **Customize Access Toolbar** dropdown button .

2. Select **More Commands** .

3. The **Excel Options** window opens to the **Customize** section, giving you access to the **Customize the Quick Access Toolbar** options. Here you can:

    • **Select Commands**: Select a command type from the **Choose commands from** dropdown 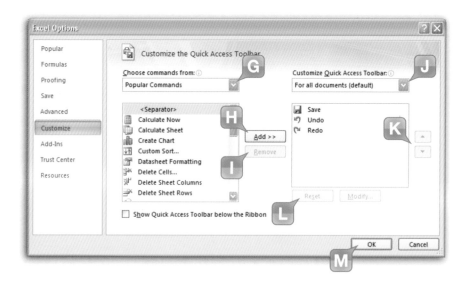, click the desired command to select it, and then click the **Add>>** button.

    • **Remove Items**: Select items in the right-hand panel and click the **Remove** button.

    • **Apply your toolbar additions/subtractions**: Make a selection to only the active worksheet or to all worksheets with the **Customize Quick Access Toolbar** dropdown.

    • **Adjust the order**: Select an item and then use the **Up** and **Down** buttons. Moving an item "up" in the list moves it left on the bar, while moving an item "down" on the list moves it right on the bar.

    • **Reset the toolbar**: Click the **Reset** button.

4. When you complete your adjustments, click the **OK** button.

Hot Tip: Adding items in this way adds them to the **Quick Access Toolbars** for *all* Microsoft Office 2007 programs. In other words, adding **New** through this dropdown in Excel will make the **New** option appear when you are working in Word and PowerPoint, as well.

Bright Idea: Minimize the Ribbon — If the ribbon takes up too much space, or you don't want to see it all the time, right-click the right tab and select, "Minimize the Ribbon". Click any tab to reveal its contents or bring the ribbon back by right clicking again and selecting"Maximize the Ribbon". Pressing CTRL + F1 on your keyboard also toggles the setting.

Quickest Click: Use this option if you want to add one of a few simple items (such as **New**, **Print Preview** and **Sort Ascending/Descending**) available in the **Customize Access Toolbar** dropdown menu. To do so, click the **Quick Access Toolbar** dropdown button and then click an item to select it.

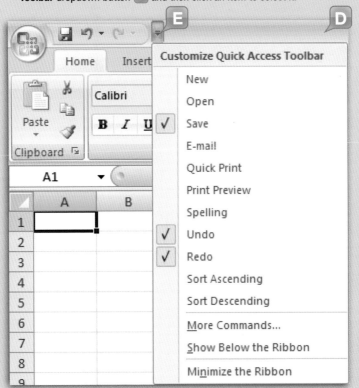

Customize the Quick Access Toolbar 163

53 | Choose What is Transferred When You Cut/Copy and Paste

Difficulty: ●○○○

There are times when you want to copy or cut and paste only some of the contents of a cell. For example, you need to move some data from a worksheet and paste it into another sheet with a different format. If you want to keep the new format, you need to use **Paste Special**.

Paste Special's capabilities are not limited to formatting and cell values. The **Paste Special** dialog box allows you to transport formulas, comments and links to external data sources, skip blank cells in pasted ranges, and control column width.

SEE ALSO APPENDIX D FOR A LIST OF KEYBOARD SHORTCUTS TO ACCESS PASTE SPECIAL

What Microsoft Calls It: Paste Special

	A	B	C
1	Old Product Numbers	Replacement Product Numbers	Final Product Number List
2	W-OW-3341	W-OW-5629	W-OW-3341
3	M-OW-4502		M-OW-4502
4	W-OW-3236		W-OW-3236
5	M-OW - 4209	M-OW-6620	M-OW - 4209
6	W-OW - 3001	W-OW-5130	M-OW - 3001
7	M-OW - 4923		
8	W-OW - 3387	W-O	

	A	B	C
1	Old Product Numbers	Replacement Product Numbers	Final Product Number List
2	W-OW-3341	W-OW-5629	W-OW-3341
3	M-OW-4502		M-OW-4502
4	W-OW-3236		W-OW-3236
5	M-OW - 4209	M-OW-6620	M-OW - 4209
6	W-OW - 3001	W-OW-5130	W-OW - 3001
7	M-OW - 4923		M-OW - 4923
8	W-OW - 3387		W-OW - 3387

Step-by-Step

Paste Special
command can paste
cell values, skipping
blanks and using
the destination cell
formatting.

1. Select the data you
   want to copy 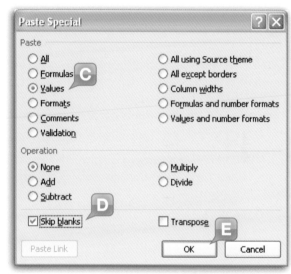A.

2. Copy the content.

3. Select the
   destination area B.

4. Right-click the
   destination area and
   select **Paste Special**.

5. In the **Paste Special** dialog box, click the **Values** radio button C (to
   insure that only the cell values, not the cell formats, are pasted). If you
   have blanks, consider clicking the **Skip Blanks** checkbox D (it will ignore
   the blank cells in the copied area and not replace those product numbers
   with blank fields).

6. Click the **OK**
   button E.

7. Review the
   destination
   selection F to be
   sure the data is
   what you intended
   to paste.

	A	B	C
1	**Old Product Numbers**	**Replacement Product Numb** F	**Final Product Number List**
2	W-OW-3341	W-OW-5629	W-OW-5629
3	M-OW-4502		M-OW-4502
4	W-OW-3236		W-OW-3236
5	M-OW - 4209	M-OW-6620	M-OW-6620
6	W-OW - 3001	W-OW-5130	W-OW-5130
7	M-OW - 4923		M-OW - 4923
8	W-OW - 3387		W-OW - 3387

STOP

54 Save a Workbook as a Template

Difficulty:

If you create the same report on a monthly, weekly, or daily basis, it might be easier to create a template rather than re-creating the same worksheet each time.

Saving a document as a template means that each time you open it you are actually creating a new copy that you can fill in or customize.

There are three separate template formats available in Excel 2007.

- **.XLTX:** This is a standard 2007 Excel template.
- **.XLTM:** This is a macro-enabled 2007 Excel template. If the workbook you are saving as a template contains macros, you will want to save it in this format.
- **.XLT:** This is the 97-2003 template format. 💡

Step-by-Step

Save a Workbook as a Template

1. Open the workbook you want to save as a template. Make sure you have deleted all of the information you do not want saved in your template version.

2. Click the **Office Button** A.

3. Click on **Save As** B.

4. Click the **Other Formats** option C.

5. Type a name for your new template in the **File Name** textbox .

6. Select **Excel Template** (or one of the other template formats) from the **Save as type** dropdown **E**.

7. Click the **Save** button **F**.

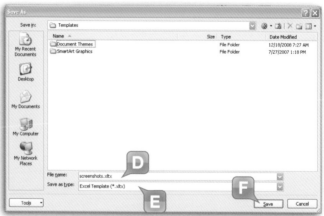

Bright Idea: Before you create your own template from scratch, check out the templates that come with 2007 or the ones available for download from Microsoft's website. To access these ready-made templates, click the **Office** button and then **New**. In the left navigation pane of the **New Workbook** window, click **Installed Templates** and browse for one you like. For downloadable content, click a category under **Office Online** and see if any of those will apply.

55 | Create Your Own Fillable List of Items

Difficulty:

Sometimes the default lists (i.e. days of the week, months of the year) do not meet your AutoFill needs. Perhaps you have a list of offices or sales regions, business or academic time units (quarters, semesters, or trimesters), or a set of products or names that you need to enter repeatedly. Instead of typing each entry or even copying and pasting, you can create a customized AutoFill list.

C	D	E
Region 1 - Northeast	Fall Semester	Store 403 - Orlando
Region 2 - Southwest	Midterm 1	Store 709 - Kansas City
Region 3 - Upper Midwest	Fall Finals	Store 992 -Chicago
Region 4 - Gulf Coast	Spring Semester	Store 1123 - San Francisco
Region 5 - Central Plains	Midterm 2	Store 77 - New York
Region 6 - Northwest	Spring Finals	Store 804 - Seattle
Region 7 - Alaska/Hawaii	Summer Term	Store 634 - Omaha
Region 8 - Eastern Canada	Midterm 3	Store 761 - Detroit
Region 9 - Western Canada	Summer Finals	Store 1094 - Phoenix

> **What Microsoft Calls It:** Create custom AutoFill series

Step-by-Step

Create your own AutoFill Series

1. Select the cells which contain the data you want to comprise your custom list .

	A	B	C
1	Store	Manager	Q1 Sales
2	Store 403 - Orlando	John Smith	$ 336,723.00
3	Store 709 - Kansas City	Jamie Wilson	$ 887,309.00
4	Store 992 -Chicago	Edward Cavanaugh	$ 228,476.00
5	Store 1123 - San Francisco	Bob Harper	$ 884,627.00
6	Store 77 - New York	Crystal Cogan	$ 205,737.00
7	Store 804 - Seattle	Jason Polito	$ 231,058.00
8	Store 634 - Omaha	Wendy Yaroch	$ 105,837.00
9	Store 761 - Detroit	Liza Bedgood	$ 847,265.00
10	Store 1094 - Phoenix	Steven Pence	$ 948,375.00

2. Click the **Office Button**.

3. Click the **Excel Options** button.

4. Select **Popular** 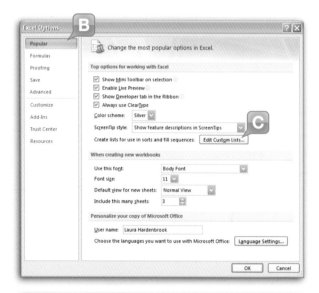 in the left navigation pane.

5. Click the **Edit Custom Lists** button to open the **Custom Lists** dialog box. This will also close the **Excel Options** window.

6. Click on the **Import** button to import your selection as a list.

7. Click the **OK** button.

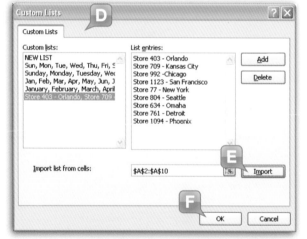

 Bright Idea: To use your custom list, place your cursor in a cell, type the first item in the list, and then click and drag the **Fill Handle**.

56 | Use AutoFill to Quickly Fill Cells from a List

Difficulty: ●○○○

Sometimes you need to enter a series of data into a set of cells. The series might be dates, numbers, times, or some other repeated list of items. Typing each item might take a very long time.

AutoFill takes a partially completed series, say three sequential months of the year, and easily extends it as long as you like. You can even take a more complex format—like the month and the year—and extend it out for years to come.

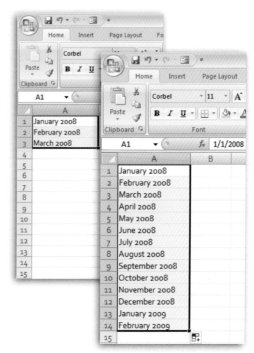

 Step-by-Step

Extend a Series of Data with AutoFill

1. Type in at least three initial values for the series.

2. Select the cells containing the three initial values 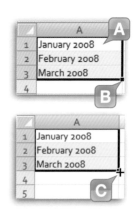.

3. Click on the **Fill Handle** when your cursor becomes a cross.

4. Drag to the desired number of cells and release.

 Option: Click on the **AutoFill** button that appears at the end of your series 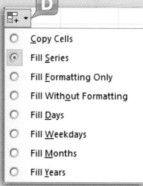 and select one of the options:

- **Copy Cells:** Changes all the cells to a copy of the initial values. January, February, March becomes a repeated series of January, February March.

- **Fill Series:** Fills a series of data based on the pattern from the initial values. January, February, March becomes January, February, March, April, etc. Repeats at January.

- **Fill Formatting:** Applies the formatting from the initial values onto all the series cells.

- **Fill Without Formatting:** Changes the contents of the cells without changing the formatting of the destination cells. If the initial cells have yellow backgrounds, and the filled cells have blue backgrounds, the filled cells will contain the series data, but will retain their blue backgrounds.

- **Fill Days, Weekdays, Months, and Years:** These four options appear depending on what kind of information is in your initial data. Days of the week will only provide **Fill Days** and **Fill Weekdays** options, while complete dates (MM/DD/YYYY) will give all options. Selecting any item will fill in date information as described by the Fill name, starting at the beginning date. A beginning data set of Monday, January 5; Tuesday, January 6; Wednesday, January 7; will yield only the days Monday through Friday, skipping Saturday and Sunday, with the correct dates.

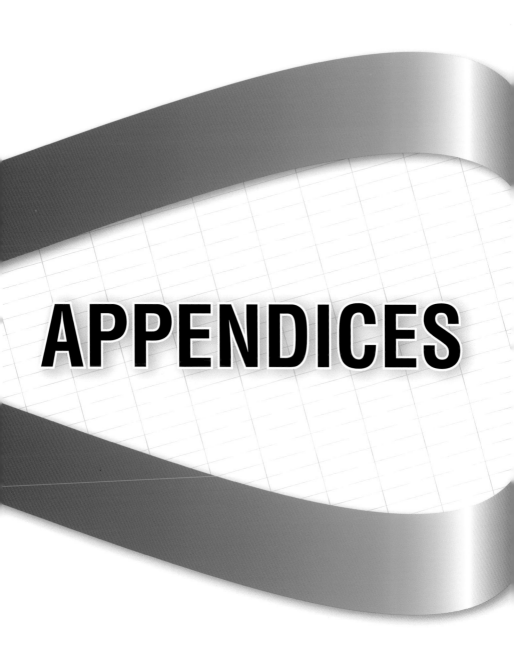

APPENDICES

A | Excel or Access: Which Do I Need?

What is the Difference Between Microsoft Excel and Microsoft Access?

In order to understand the difference between two types of databases, you first need to understand what a database really is. While we usually think of databases as being electronic, take a look at some paper-based information that could technically be considered a database.

- A phone list address book
- A collection of documents
- A rolodex of business cards

An electronic database can take many forms as well. A list of information in a Word table, an Excel spreadsheet, and an Access file can all be considered databases. Some of the most common uses for databases include:

- Managing products, pricing, and inventory
- Tracking sales
- Keeping employee information
- Managing invoices, payments, or expenses

The two basic kinds of databases are "flat" and "relational." In a flat database, all the information is contained in a single table, and each record contains a single reference and associated pieces of data. In other words, your left-most column contains an identifier, like a person's name, and each column in that person's row contains information about that person, such as address and telephone number. A paper phone book is a great example of a flat database. The listings appear in alphabetical order by the person's last name, which is the "reference." The pieces of information, such as first name, address, and phone number, would be in columns in the person's record.

A relational database takes the information a step further. It places information in multiple tables and then hooks them together when you need them. In a relational database, the information is stored in several related tables. This works best when you have certain information that is used over and over again. The information is spread out into tables so that it only has to be entered and maintained in one place. This makes it easier to enter, easier to update, and less likely to have errors.

Microsoft Access is software specifically designed to serve as a database. It has special features and functions that programs like Word or Excel do not have. Some of the differences include the fact that Access is a multi-user program, while only one person at a time can work on an Excel spreadsheet or Word document. This makes Access a great choice for company-wide information such as product or sales data. Several can be entering data at once, and others can be looking data up at the same time. Probably the biggest reason to use Access over other software is that it is a relational database. A relational database separates out information into tables so that it only has to be entered and maintained in one place. This makes it easier to enter, easier to update, and less likely to have errors.

When Would I Use Access Instead of Excel?

Let's say you run a food services company and you have a database that contains information about your supplies. Each product has a supplier and a category. These suppliers and categories are found on several different items. In a spreadsheet or other flat database, information is in each line. The challenge, however, would come when that information needed to be updated. If you change the name of the Condiments category to Sauces, you would need to change it on every single item. However, in a relational database, similar information is grouped into its own table, then linked with the other tables. You can create one table to show categories, another table to show suppliers. Then link both of those tables to the Products table. When you change the name of the category in its own table, it is updated everywhere automatically — no more redundant data entry.

The same kind of linking can be done with the supplier's address. That address is used many different ways. It appears on many different requisitions and invoices. You could enter it each time on each requisition, or put that in one table and link it to the others. Not only does it save data entry time, but it also reduces errors. If you had to type the address in 15 different places, there is a good chance there might be an error in at least one of them. Even a single error can make it difficult to search for information or pull reports later since the information is entered slightly differently for that entry.

Here is a table that identifies some key features and business needs and then illustrates how they are handled by each program. Use this chart (and other resources) to review your needs and decide which program is best for you.

Key Feature	Microsoft Access 2007	Microsoft Excel 2007	Additional Notes
Storage Capacity	★	★	Both Microsoft Excel and Microsoft Access can store a great deal of data and a large number of records.
Security	★	★	Both Microsoft Excel and Microsoft Access provide a wide range of security measures across multiple levels.
Multiple Data Relationships	★	★	Microsoft Excel stores data in a "flat" environment, while Microsoft Access is a "relational" database that allows one-to-one and one-to-many relationships.
Non-Textual/ Non-Numeric Data Formats	★	★	Microsoft Excel stores numbers and text. Microsoft Access can store formatted, or "Rich" text, graphics, or even entire documents.
Multiple Users	★	☆	Microsoft Excel provides for basic sharing and collaboration on worksheets. Microsoft Access allows several users to access the same data simultaneously and includes information flow management options.
Consolidate Data from Multiple Sources	★	☆	Microsoft Excel can pull data from a web page or network location when you manually direct it to do so. Microsoft Access can be linked directly to external data sources for continuous and automatic data retrieval.
Create Visualizations of Data	☆	★	Microsoft Access can be used to generate reports and has simple conditional formatting options. Microsoft Excel allows you to produce charts and graphs, allows for robust conditional formatting, allows the use of SmartArt and can export information directly to PowerPoint.

Key Feature	Microsoft Access 2007	Microsoft Excel 2007	Additional Notes
On-Demand Data Manipulation			Microsoft Access gives you some ability to manipulate data via table views and reports. Microsoft Excel allows you to review and "tweak" variables in tables, PivotTables, and PivotCharts and review the consequences of your changes in real-time.
Formulas, Functions and Calculations			Microsoft Access allows you to program calculations and to run some formulas in particular sections of your database. Microsoft Excel provides a wide range of analysis tools, calculations, and functions that work on all sections of your workbook.

 Performs well   Performs but with some limitations   Does not perform

B

Chart Terminology

Here are some terms you will need to keep in mind when working with charts.

Chart Axes: Charts generally have two axes—an X axis and a Y axis. The Y axis usually represents the categories of data in a chart, while the X axis usually represents the range of possible values that are being charted.

In this chart, a company has three offices—Beaumont, Regency, and Edwardsville. Each office needs to order supplies for their office—wall calendars, employee handbooks, ledgers, and planners. The Y axis categories— the items to be ordered—are in column A of the table and along the bottom of the chart. The reference points on the X axis, along the left border of the chart, are derived from the information in columns B, C, and D of the PivotTable. Those X axis numbers give a guideline to help viewers of the chart read the data.

Values: Values are the data line-items tracked on the chart. In this case, each value from column B is represented by a colored pillar in the chart. The height of the pillar corresponds with the X axis reference points to show the relationship between the graphed items.

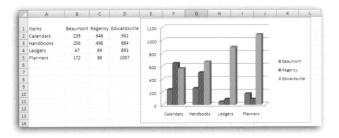

Legends: Legends are tables to help you read charts. By default, the legend on the right identifies how each piece of data is tracked (line, bar, etc.) and/or the color associated with it. In this example, the legend shows that the blue pillars on the chart represent the Beaumont office orders, the red represent the Regency office orders, and the green represent the Edwardsville office orders.

Which Chart for Which Data

Select the best chart type and format to present your data in the most meaningful way. If you need assistance in selecting the right chart for your needs use the Chart Advisor to help you select your chart. Chart Advisor is a wizard that scans your data and makes a chart selection for you. In order to use Chart Advisor you will need to install the Chart Advisor from Microsoft's Office Labs site, but once it is installed you can access it from the **Insert** tab within the Office Labs panel. You can download Chart Advisor from: **http://www.officelabs.com/projects/chartadvisor/Pages/default.aspx**

Chart Types

The following is a description of the major chart types available with some suggested uses.

Column: The column chart puts fixed data in a visual format. Categories appear horizontally and values appear vertically. Variations include the cylinder, cone, and pyramid chart subtypes.

	A	B	C	D
1	Items	Beaumont	Regency	Edwardsville
2	Calendars	239	646	562
3	Handbooks	256	498	664
4	Ledgers	47	89	893
5	Planners	172	88	1087

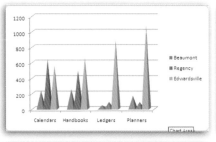
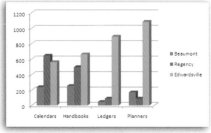
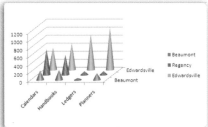
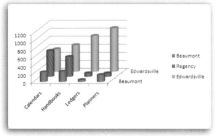

Line: A line chart shows the relationship of changes in data over a period of time. It is useful for identifying trends in data.

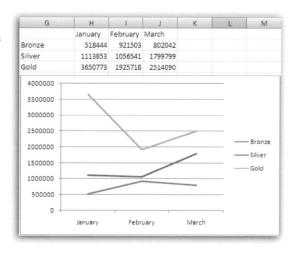

Pie: Pie charts contain just one data series. It shows the relationship of the parts to the whole. To emphasize the importance of one of the slices, select one of the exploded 2-D or 3-D pie charts.

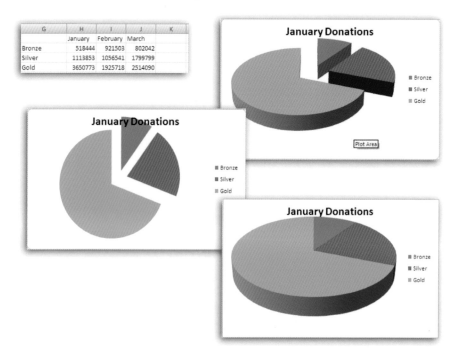

Bar: A horizontal bar chart compares items at a fixed period of time. This chart type also includes cylinder, cone, and pyramid subtypes.

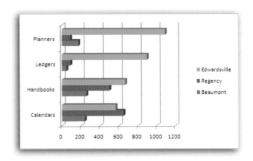

Area: An area chart shows the relative importance of values over time. Similar to a line chart, it emphasizes the magnitude of values more so than the line chart.

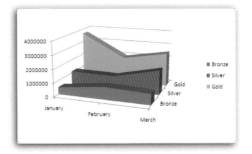

XY (Scatter): Scatter charts show a correlation among data points that might not be easy to see from raw data. It uses numeric values along both axes instead of values along the vertical axis and categories along the horizontal axis.

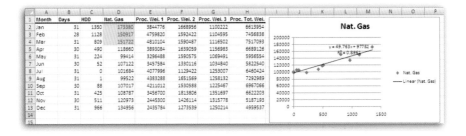

C Formulas and Functions

The Language of Formulas and Functions

Excel makes it a simple task to perform mathematical operations. Using formulas, you can calculate and analyze data in your worksheet. Formulas are equations that combine values and cell references with operators to calculate a result. Functions are prebuilt formulas that can be quickly fed values without the need to write the underlying formula yourself. But to use either you need to know how to write in their own language, which is commonly referred to as **operators**. And, like any language, operators have their own form of grammar, referred to as **Order of Precedence**.

Operators used in Formulas and Functions

Mathematical Operators

To perform basic mathematical operations such as addition, subtraction, or multiplication; combine numbers; and produce numeric results, use the following arithmetic operators.

Arithmetic operator		Meaning	Example
Plus Sign	+	Addition	=(B2+C2+D2)

	A	B	C	D	E	F
					Total	
1	Items	Beaumont	Regency	Edwardsville	Needed	Ordered
2	Calendars	239	646	562	1447	1500
3	Handbooks	256	498	664	1418	1500
4	Ledgers	47	89	893	1029	1100
5	Planners	172	88	1087	1347	1400

Arithmetic operator		Meaning	Example
Minus Sign	-	Subtraction	=(B2+C2-D2)

	A	B	C	D	E	F
					Total	
1	Items	Beaumont	Regency	Edwardsville	Needed	Ordered
2	Calendars	239	646	562	323	400
3	Handbooks	256	498	664	1418	1500
4	Ledgers	47	89	893	1029	1100
5	Planners	172	88	1087	1347	1400

Arithmetic operator		Meaning	Example
Minus Sign	-	Negation	=−(B2+C2-D2)

	A	B	C	D	E	F
1	Items	Beaumont	Regency	Edwardsville	Total Needed	Ordered
2	Calendars	239	646	562	-323	-400
3	Handbooks	256	498	664	1418	1500
4	Ledgers	47	89	893	1029	1100
5	Planners	172	88	1087	1347	1400

Arithmetic operator		Meaning	Example
Asterisk	*	Multiplication	=2*(A2+C2-D2)

	A	B	C	D	E	F
1	Items	Beaumont	Regency	Edwardsville	Total Needed	Ordered
2	Calendars	239	646	562	2894	2900
3	Handbooks	256	498	664	1418	1500
4	Ledgers	47	89	893	1029	1100
5	Planners	172	88	1087	1347	1400

Arithmetic operator		Meaning	Example
Forward Slash	/	Division	=(B2+C2-D2)/2

	A	B	C	D	E	F
1	Items	Beaumont	Regency	Edwardsville	Total Needed	Ordered
2	Calendars	239	646	562	723.5	800
3	Handbooks	256	498	664	1418	1500
4	Ledgers	47	89	893	1029	1100
5	Planners	172	88	1087	1347	1400

Arithmetic operator		Meaning	Example
Percent Sign	%	Percent	=(B2 + C2 - D2)*20%

	A	B	C	D	E	F
1	Items	Beaumont	Regency	Edwardsville	Total Needed	Ordered
2	Calendars	239	646	562	289.4	300
3	Handbooks	256	498	664	1418	1500
4	Ledgers	47	89	893	1029	1100
5	Planners	172	88	1087	1347	1400

Arithmetic operator		Meaning	Example
Caret	^	Exponentiation (squared[2], cubed[3], etc.)	=(B2+C2+D2)^2

	A	B	C	D	E	F
1	Items	Beaumont	Regency	Edwardsville	Total Needed	Ordered
2	Calendars	239	646	562	2093809	2093900
3	Handbooks	256	498	664	1418	1500
4	Ledgers	47	89	893	1029	1100
5	Planners	172	88	1087	1347	1400

Comparison Operators

You can compare two values with the following operators. When two values are compared by using these operators, the result is a logical value, either TRUE or FALSE.

	F2		fx =(C2=D2)			
	A	B	C	D	E	F
1	Comparison Operator	Symbol	Number 1	Number 2	Formula	Result
2	Equal To	=	8	8	=(A2=B2)	TRUE
3		=	9	8	=(A3=B3)	FALSE
4	Greater Than	>	9	8	=(A3>B3)	TRUE
5		>	8	9	=(A5>B5)	FALSE
6	Less Than	<	9	8	=(C6<D6)	FALSE
7		<	8	9	=(C7<D7))	TRUE
8	Greater Than or Equal To	>=	9	8	=(C8>=D8)	TRUE
9		>=	8	8	=(C9>=D9)	TRUE
10		>=	8	9	=(C10>=D10)	FALSE
11	Less Than or Equal To	<=	8	9	=(C11<=D11)	TRUE
12		<=	8	8	=(C12<=D12)	TRUE
13		<=	9	8	=(C13<=D13)	FALSE
14	Not Equal To	<>	9	8	=(C14<>C15)	TRUE
15		<>	8	8	=(C15<>D15)	FALSE

Text Concatenation Operator

Use the ampersand (&) to join, or concatenate, one or more text strings to produce a single piece of text.

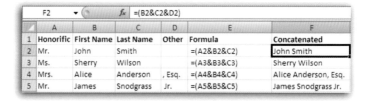

	F2		fx =(B2&C2&D2)			
	A	B	C	D	E	F
1	Honorific	First Name	Last Name	Other	Formula	Concatenated
2	Mr.	John	Smith		=(A2&B2&C2)	John Smith
3	Ms.	Sherry	Wilson		=(A3&B3&C3)	Sherry Wilson
4	Mrs.	Alice	Anderson	, Esq.	=(A4&B4&C4)	Alice Anderson, Esq.
5	Mr.	James	Snodgrass	Jr.	=(A5&B5&C5)	James Snodgrass Jr.

Order of Precedence in which Excel Performs Operations

The order in which a calculation is performed affects the result, so it is important to understand how the order is determined and how you can change it to obtain desired results.

A formula in Excel always begins with an equal sign (=). The equal sign tells Excel that the succeeding characters are part of a formula or function. After the equal sign are the elements to be calculated (the operands), which are separated by calculation operators. Excel calculates from left to right, using the PEMDAS (Parentheses, Exponents, Multiplication, Division, Addition, Subtraction) order of operations. In other words, it performs calculations in parentheses first, then it checks for multiplication and division, then finally it performs addition and subtraction. Using these rules of math is what makes it possible to do some potentially confusing problems that have many possible results if you do not follow the right order. Knowing that this is how Excel reads math, you need to structure your formulas accordingly.

$$2+3x4-5/6=?$$

If this problem were performed just from left to right, the answer would be "2.5."

However, your intent might have been very different. Adding parentheses to show which items should be calculated first helps.

$$(2+(3x4)-5)/6$$

This same set of numbers with parentheses added calculate to a much different total. 3x4 is calculated first, for a total of 12. 2 is added to get 14, from which 5 is subtracted to get 9. Finally, 9 is divided by 6 for a total of 1.5.

D | Keyboard Shortcuts

Selection and Editing

Shift+F8 . . . . .Adds other nonadjacent cells or ranges to the selection

Shift+F8 . . . . .Adds to the selection (toggle)

Esc . . . . .Cancels the editing

Ctrl+Del . . . . .Deletes all characters from the cursor to the end of the line

Backspace . . . . . . .Deletes the character to the left of the cursor

Del . . . . .Deletes the character to the right of the cursor

Shift+F10 . . . . . . .Opens and Displays a shortcut menu

Shift+F2 . . . . .Edits a cell comment

F2. . . . . .Edits the active cell

Ctrl+C . . . . .Copies the selected cell contents

Ctrl+X . . . . .Cuts the selected cell contents

Ctrl+D . . . . .Fills Down

Ctrl+R . . . . .Fills Right

Ctrl+F . . . . .Find

Ctrl+V . . . . .Paste

Ctrl+H . . . . .Launches the Replace dialog box

Ctrl+Z . . . . .Same as clicking the Undo button

Ctrl+N . . . . .Opens a New document

Ctrl+O . . . . .Launches the File Open dialog box

Ctrl+P . . . . .Prints

Ctrl+S . . . . .Saves

Alt+' . . . . .Launches the Style dialog box

Ctrl+K . . . . .Launches the Insert Hyperlink dialog box

Alt+F4 . . . . .Exits the program

Shift+arrow key . . .Expands the selection in the direction indicated

Shift+Home . . . . .Expands the selection to the beginning of the current row

F8. . . . . .Extends the selection as navigation keys are used

Shift+F4 . . . . . . .Repeats the last Find (Find Next)

Formatting

Ctrl+Shift+& . . . . .Adds border to outline

Ctrl+Shift+! . . . . .Adds the comma format with two decimal places

Ctrl+Shift+$ . . . . .Adds the currency format with two decimal places

Ctrl+Shift+# . . . . .Adds the date format (day, month, year)

Ctrl+Shift+~ . . . . .Adds the general number format

Ctrl+Shift+%. . . . .Adds the percent format with no decimal places

Ctrl+Shift+@. . . . .Adds the time format (hour, minute, a.m./p.m.)

Ctrl+B . . . . .Sets or removes boldface

Ctrl+I. . . . . .Sets or removes italic

Ctrl+5 . . . . .Sets or removes strikethrough

Ctrl+U . . . . .Sets or removes underlining

Ctrl+Shift+_ . . . . .Removes all borders

Navigation and Display

Ctrl+F4 . . . . .Closes the window

Ctrl+6 . . . . .Cycles through the ways to display objects

Ctrl+F3 . . . . .Defines a name

Ctrl+Alt+F9 . . . . .Global calculation

Ctrl+0 (zero) . . . . .Hides columns

Ctrl+9 . . . . .Hides rows

Alt+F1 . . . . .Inserts a chart sheet

Alt+Shift+F1 . . . . .Inserts a new worksheet

Shift+F11 . . . . . .Inserts a new worksheet

Ctrl+Shift+F3 . . . .Opens and Displays the Creates Names dialog box

Shift+F5 . . . . . . .Opens and Displays the Find dialog box

Ctrl+1 . . . . .Opens and Displays the Format dialog box for the selected object

F5. . . . . .Opens and Displays the Go To dialog box

Alt+F8 . . . . . . .Opens and Displays the Macro dialog box

Shift+F1 . . . . . . .Opens and Displays the What's This cursor

Alt+F11. . . . . . . .Opens and Displays Visual Basic Editor

Ctrl+F12 . . . . . . .Prompts Open command

Ctrl+Shift+F12. . . .Prompts Print command

Alt+F2 . . . . .Prompts Save As command

F12 . . . . .Prompts Save As command

Alt+Shift+F2 . . . . .Prompts Save command

F7. . . . . .Prompts Spelling command

F10 . . . . .Makes the menu bar active

Ctrl+F10 . . . . . . .Maximizes or restores the workbook window

Ctrl+F9 . . . . . . .Minimizes the workbook

PgDn . . . . .Moves down one screen

Alt+PgUp. . . . . . .Moves one screen to the left

Alt+PgDn. . . . . . .Moves one screen to the right

Shift+Tab. . . . . . .Moves the cell pointer left to the preceding cell in the selection

Tab . . . . .Moves the cell pointer right to the next cell

Ctrl+. (period) . . . .Moves the cell pointer to the next corner of the current cell range

Shift+Enter. . . . . .Moves the cell pointer up to the preceding cell in the selection

Arrow keys. . . . . .Moves the cursor one character in the direction of the arrow

Ctrl+left arrow . . . .In edit mode, moves the cursor one word to the left

Ctrl+right arrow . . . Moves the cursor one word to the right

End . . . . .Moves the cursor to the end of the line

F1. . . . . .Opens and Displays Help or the Office Assistant

F2. . . . . .Begins editing the active cell

F3. . . . . .Pastes a name into a formula

F4. . . . . .Repeats the last action

F6. . . . . .Moves to the next pane

F8. . . . . .Extends the selection as navigation keys are used

F9. . . . . .Calculates all sheets in all open workbooks

F10 . . . . .Makes the menu bar active

F11 . . . . .Creates a chart

F12 . . . . .Issues Save As command

Home. . . . . . . .Moves to the beginning of the row

Ctrl+arrow key. . . .Moves to the edge of a data block

Ctrl+Home . . . . . .Moves to the first cell in the worksheet (A1)

Ctrl+End . . . . . . .Moves to the last active cell of the worksheet

End* . . . . .Moves to the lower-left cell displayed in the window

               *When the scroll lock is active

Ctrl+PgDn . . . . . .Moves to the next sheet

Ctrl+F6. . . . . . . .Moves to the next window

Ctrl+Tab . . . . . . .Moves to the next window

Shift+F6 . . . . . . .Moves to the previous pane of a window that has been split

Ctrl+PgUp . . . . . .Moves to the previous sheet

Ctrl+Shift+Tab. . . .Moves to the previous window

Ctrl+Shift+F6 . . . .Moves to the previous workbook window

Home* . . . . .Moves to the upper-left cell displayed in the window

               *When the scroll lock is active

PgUp . . . . .Moves up one screen

Ctrl+F8 . . . . .Resizes the window

Ctrl+F5 . . . . .Restores the window size

Arrow keys. . . . . .Scrolls left, right, up, or down one cell

Ctrl+Backspace . . .Scrolls to display the active cell

Ctrl+A . . . . .Selects all

Shift+Backspace . .Selects the active cell in a range selection

Ctrl+* . . . . .Selects the block of data surrounding the active cell

Ctrl+Space . . . . . .Selects the entire column(s) in the selected range

Shift+Space . . . . .Selects the entire row(s) in the selected range

Ctrl+Shift+ Space . .Selects the entire worksheet

Alt+Enter. . . . . . .Starts a new line in the current cell

Ctrl+8 . . . . .Toggles the display of outline symbols

Ctrl+Shift+) . . . . .Unhides columns

Ctrl+Shift+(. . . . .Unhides rows

Formulas and Functions

Ctrl+: . . . . .Enters the current date

Ctrl+Shift+: . . . . .Enters the current time

Alt+= . . . . .Inserts the AutoSum formula

Shift+F3 . . . . . . .Pastes a function into a formula

Ctrl+G . . . . .Prompts for a range or range name to select

The "Magic" ALT Key

When you press the ALT key on your keyboard, letters appear on the ribbon. Clicking a letter launches the corresponding function. Unlike other keyboard shortcuts, ALT shortcut keys are pressed sequentially, not held down at once. This can be much faster than using the mouse. Here are some basic ALT shortcuts for you to use.

Alt+E+S+T . . . . . .Opens the Paste Special dialog box with the **Formats** radio button selected

Alt+E+S+V . . . . . .Opens the Paste Special dialog box with the **Values** radio button selected

Alt+E+S+F . . . . . . Opens the Paste Special dialog box with the **Formulas** radio button selected

Alt+E+S+C . . . . . . Opens the Paste Special dialog box with the **Comments** radio button selected

Alt+E+S+N . . . . . . Opens the Paste Special dialog box with the **Validation** radio button selected

Alt+E+S+H . . . . . . Opens the Paste Special dialog box with the **All using Source theme** radio button selected

Alt+E+S+X . . . . . . Opens the Paste Special dialog box with the **All except borders** radio button selected

Alt+E+S+W . . . . . Opens the Paste Special dialog box with the **Column Widths** radio button selected

Alt+E+S+R . . . . . . Opens the Paste Special dialog box with the **Formulas and number formats** radio button selected

Alt+E+S+U . . . . . . Opens the Paste Special dialog box with the **Values and number formats** radio button selected

Alt+E+S+R . . . . . . Opens the Paste Special dialog box with the **Formulas and number formats** radio button selected

Alt+E+S+U . . . . . . Opens the Paste Special dialog box with the **Values and number formats** radio button selected

Alt+E+S+A . . . . . . Opens the Paste Special dialog box with the **All** radio button selected

Alt+E+S+A+O . . . . Opens the Paste Special dialog box with the **All** and **None** radio buttons selected

Alt+E+S+A+D . . . . Opens the Paste Special dialog box with the **All** and **Add** radio buttons selected

Alt+E+S+A+S . . . . Opens the Paste Special dialog box with the **All** and **Subtract** radio buttons selected

Alt+E+S+A+M . . . . Opens the Paste Special dialog box with the **All** and **Multiply** radio buttons selected

Alt+E+S+A+I . . . . Opens the Paste Special dialog box with the **All** and **Divide** radio buttons selected

Alt+E+S+<*>+B . . . Opens the Paste Special dialog box with the **Skip Blanks** checkbox checked *
Any letter selection

Alt+E+S+<*>+E . . . Opens the Paste Special dialog box with the **Transpose** checkbox checked *
Any letter selection

Index

A

Action Bar   2
Add-Ins Tab   3
AutoFill   168, 170, 171

C

Calculated Item   iv, 66, 67, 68, 69, 80
Cell Styles   16, 17, 18
Chart   v, 80, 106, 107, 108, 109, 110, 111, 114, 115, 116, 117, 178, 179, 180
Check for Errors   56
    See also Error Checking
Color Scales   72, 76, 77
Column Width   iv, 4, 5, 6, 7
Conditional Formatting   72, 73, 76, 78
Conditional Function   iv, 52, 53, 54, 55
Convert Text to Numbers   iv, 20, 21, 22, 23, 24, 26
Copy   iv, v, 16, 18, 19, 21, 36, 40, 41, 51, 164, 165, 171, 186
Customize Document Themes   126
Customize User Preferences   2
Custom Style   16, 17, 18
Cut   v, 164, 165, 186

D

Data Bars   72, 76
Data Filters   iv, 70, 71
Data Tab   33, 71, 153
Define a Constant   30
Dependents   58, 59
    See also Trace Precedents and Dependents
Developer Tab   98, 99, 101, 103

E

Error Checking   56
    See also Check for Errors
Excel Options   ix, 2, 98, 162, 168, 169
External Data Source   152
External Reference Links   144

F

Fill Handle   40, 169, 170
Footers   128, 129, 131, 132

F (continued)

Format Menu   4, 6, 186
Formula   iv, ix, 35, 36, 37, 38, 39, 40, 41, 47, 49, 53, 54, 56, 57, 59, 65, 68, 69
Formula Autocomplete Tooltip   47, 49, 54
Formula Bar   ix, 57
Formulas Tab   31, 56, 59, 105
Freeze   iv, 10, 11
Freeze Panes   11
Functions   iv, 21, 40, 48, 49, 50, 51, 56, 57
Function Wizard   48

H

Headers   ix, 128
Headers and Footers   128, 129
Hide   iv, 8, 9
Home Tab   6, 9, 14, 15, 16, 17, 18, 23, 24, 26, 43, 71, 73, 76, 78, 103, 126

I

Icon Sets   72
Insert Tab   81, 108, 115, 119, 126, 128, 149, 179

L

Link Worksheets   v, 144, 145, 146, 147

M

Macro   v, 13, 98, 99, 100, 101, 102, 103, 188
Mail Merge   156, 157, 158, 159
Merge   iv, 14, 15, 18, 156, 157, 158, 159
Merge and Split   14

N

Named Cell   30
Named Cells and Ranges   104
Named Range   30, 104

O

Office Button   2, 98, 160, 167

P

Page Break Preview   141, 142, 143
Page Layout Tab   123, 126, 127, 130, 137, 139, 140, 142

Page Setup   v, 130, 131, 132, 133, 134, 136, 137, 138, 139, 140, 142
Paste Special   20, 21, 164, 165, 190, 191
PivotChart   ii, 114, 115
PivotTable   ii, iv, v, 60, 61, 62, 63, 64, 65, 66, 67, 69, 80, 81, 82, 83, 84, 85, 86, 87, 88, 89, 90, 91, 92, 93, 114, 115, 116, 117, 178
Precedents   58
    See also Trace Precedents and Dependents
Print Area   v, 130, 133, 134, 135, 136, 137, 138, 139, 140, 141, 142, 143, 163, 186, 188

Q

Query   94, 152, 153
Query an External Data Source   152
Quick Access Toolbar   v, 2, 3, 103, 160, 161, 162, 163

R

Ribbon   ix, x, xi, 85, 98, 126, 163
Row Height   iv, 4, 5, 6, 7
R-squared Value   112, 113

S

Save As   12, 166, 188, 189
Set and Clear Print Area   137
SmartArt Graphic   v, 118, 119, 120, 121
Split   14, 15
Style   iv, 16, 17, 18, 186
Subtotal   iv, 32, 33, 34, 35

T

Template   v, 166, 167
Theme   v, 122, 123, 124, 125, 126, 127
Trace Precedents and Dependents   58
Trendline   110, 111, 113

U

Unfreeze   iv, 10, 11
Unhide   iv, 8, 9
Unmerge   iv, 14, 15
User Preferences   2

V

VBA   v, 13, 98, 99, 100
View Tab   11, 141
Visual Basic for Applications   98, 100, 188
VLOOKUP   94, 95, 96

W

Web Query   153
Windows Menu   ix